759.949   E97a   FV   C.
EYCK
ALL THE PAINTINGS OF
JAN VAN EYCK

WITHDRAWN

BK   759.949   E97A
ALL THE PAINTINGS OF JAN VAN EYCK   /EYCK, JAN
1962   .00   FV
3000 084215 30012
St. Louis Community College

JUN...   ...T
of S...   ...y

5545 West Park
St. Louis, Missouri 63105

 PRINTED IN U.S.A.

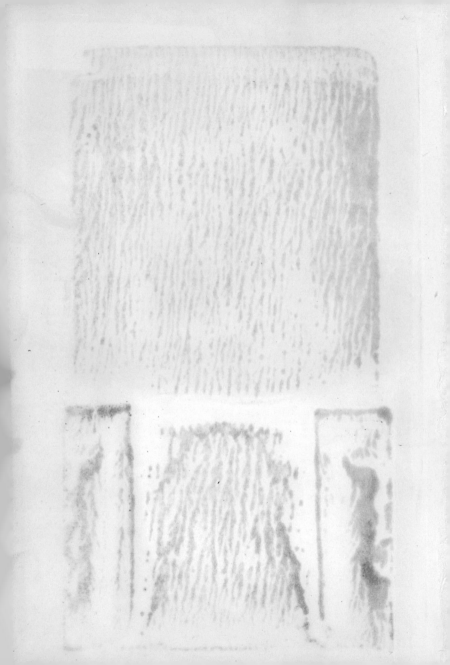

ALL THE PAINTINGS OF
JAN VAN EYCK

VOLUME FOUR
in the
Complete Library of World Art

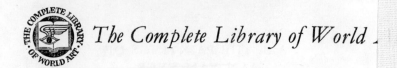

ALL THE PAINTINGS

OF JAN VAN EYCK

Text by VALENTIN DENIS
Translated by PAUL COLACICCHI

HAWTHORN BOOKS, INC.

Publishers · New York

© 1961 by Rizzoli Editore, s.p.a. All rights reserved, including the right to reproduce this book or portions thereof in any form, except for the inclusion of brief quotations in a review. All inquiries should be addressed to Hawthorn Books, Inc., 70 Fifth Avenue, New York City 11. This book is published simultaneously in Canada by McClelland & Stewart, Ltd, 25 Hollinger Road, Toronto 16. The Library of Congress has catalogued this volume of *The Complete Library of World Art* under card number 62–10518. Suggested decimal classification for this series 759.03.

Printed in Great Britain by
Jarrold & Sons Ltd, Norwich

CONTENTS

JAN VAN EYCK

Life and Work

IN the whole history of art there is possibly no problem as difficult, baffling and controversial as that concerning the two Van Eyck brothers and their respective paintings. Most of the epigraphic and literary sources seem to have conspired to deepen the confusion. From the end of the sixteenth century onwards, these sources and the artists' works have been interpreted regardless of the main principles of historical criticism. This critique seeks to place the situation in its proper perspective, with a maximum of objectivity, keeping in mind only the authenticated facts. Jan Van Eyck's work deserves such admiration that we cannot allow it to be dimmed by legendary or hypothetical tales about an elusive brother, and by the attribution of works unworthy of his status.

Everything leads us to believe that Jan Van Eyck was born in the valley of the Meuse (Limburg), at Maastricht, or in that neighborhood. Some ancient biographers—Lucas de Heere (1565) and Marcus van Vaernewijck (1568)—place his birth in Maaseik, but this assumption is not confirmed by records of Van Eyck's time. The inference was probably derived from the artist's surname and from the fact that his daughter Livina, who became a nun in 1449, elected to go to a convent in Maaseik: her choice—she was a native of Ghent—could only lead one to assume that she may have had some family connexions in the Meuse area—nothing more.

7

On the other hand, Van Eyck's motto, *Als ich can* ("As I can"), and his own notes on the preparatory drawings for the portrait of Cardinal Albergati (Dresden), which seem to echo the Flemish *patois* of the Belgian-Dutch region of Limburg, rich with Germanic inflections, have led Antonio de Beatis and others to believe—mistakenly—that Van Eyck was German born. Nor is the date of the artist's birth precisely known. It has been established that in 1682, Diego Duarte, who lived at Antwerp, owned a Van Eyck picture dated 1414; from this one may argue that Jan was born about 1390 and that he was over forty years of age at the time of his marriage in 1434.

Thanks to existing records, his life can be traced in its broader lines from October 24, 1422, when he is known to have been at The Hague in the service of John of Bavaria, Count of Holland, who died on January 5, 1425; on May 19 of the following year Van Eyck became the faithful servant and court painter of that powerful Prince and enlightened patron of the arts, Philip the Good, Duke of Burgundy, who treated him with great affection and frequently employed him on missions of trust. When the Duke's second wife—Bonne d'Artois, whom he had married after the death of Michelle of France—died, he despatched an official delegation to Lisbon to beg the hand of Isabella of Portugal (October 1428), and Jan Van Eyck joined the mission, headed by Jean de Roubaix, in order to paint the Princess's portrait for his master, to whom he sent the finished picture on February 12, 1429. He was invited to the wedding, which took place at Sluus on January 7, 1430.

After many repeated journeys between Lille and the Castle of Hesdin and elsewhere in the wake of a Duke who was always in the saddle, Van Eyck settled at Bruges in 1431, and later bought a house in that city. His

8

growing reputation earned him a visit by the town's Chief Magistrate (1432) and by Philip himself (1433); in fact, the Duke was god-father at the christening of the artist's first child, born in June 1434. Later he was to increase the artist's salary, to make him a present of six silver goblets and to bestow upon him many other precious gifts and honors to reward him for his fine works.

Famous at home and abroad, Van Eyck now began to sign his paintings: nine of his panels, completed between 1432 and 1439, bear his name and a date—an exceptional practice for northern Europe at the time. He died in Bruges on July 9, 1441, and was buried in the church of St Donatian, a building which no longer exists.

What, on the other hand, is known about his brother Hubrecht or Hubert? While the documents pertaining to Jan Van Eyck are indisputable, the records connected with Hubrecht give rise to doubts of every kind. In the Ghent archives there are four anodyne texts—for the years between 1424 and 1426—which have been strenuously upheld as the principal evidence of Hubrecht Van Eyck's existence and artistic production. The first of these documents states that a certain *Master Luberecht* provided the city's local authorities with two sketches. Elsewhere a *Master Hubrecht, painter,* is mentioned. But the surname is never mentioned and furthermore nothing suggests that the man was a painter of distinction. In the two remaining documents one does find the names, *Master Ubrechts* and *Lubrecht Van Heike*, but not a word to prove that these men were artists. Now to claim that these four references all relate to one artist, that the artist was one of the best known in the profession, and that more specifically he was Hubrecht Van Eyck, brother of Jan and, like him, a painter, would surely be to stretch beyond reasonable limits the sketchy information contained in the records.

In 1892, in Ghent, someone brought to light the "tombstone" of Hubrecht, which has since been kept in that city's Musée Lapidaire. But the tombstone is clearly decorated in late sixteenth-century style, and the epitaph referring to the artist—now lost but transcribed in 1568 by Marcus van Vaernewijck—cannot be as old as 1426 (*circa*), for its style, both literary and graphic, also recalls the second half of the sixteenth century. Van Vaernewijck himself, furthermore, admitted that this could not be an original epitaph, and that it was conceived "along the lines of the ancient Flemish *carmina*". It is surprising, too, that no one seemed to have noticed the epitaph before 1568 when for a century and a half so many visitors had flocked to the Vijdt Chapel in the Cathedral of St Bavon in Ghent to admire the *Adoration of the Sacred Lamb*. It appears, moreover, that Ghent's poet-chronicler, Lucas de Heere, did not know, as late as 1565, the date of Hubrecht's death; one must therefore conclude that the inscription on the tombstone was composed between 1565 and 1568. Nor unfortunately can one reject *a priori* the theory that De Heere, a rather imaginative writer, composed it himself. The author of the epitaph, whoever he was, acted presumably on the basis of two historical facts which may have misled him, as in the first place he appears to have accepted 1426 as the date of Hubrecht's death. Indeed, the communal archives of Ghent recorded in that year the death of a *Hubrecht Van Heycke*, but did not specify that he was a painter and the brother of the famous Jan. On the other hand local tradition would have it that the creator of the *Adoration of the Sacred Lamb* was buried at the foot of the altar in the Vijdt Chapel. This, at least, is what we gather from the Nürnberg scholar, Hieronymus Münzer, after his visit to Ghent in 1495: *Sepultus est autem magister tabellae ante altare*. One may immediately note that Hubrecht is not mentioned, but only "the master who painted the polyptych"—in other words, Jan.

Münzer was surprised to find that a painter was buried in the chapel of a rich and powerful family, a chapel, furthermore, just big enough to contain the tombs of the Vijdts. There is no doubt that Joos Vijdt, the chapel's founder and donor of the polyptych, had himself buried *ante altare* ("before the altar"), in the place that was rightfully his and his alone. One may assume, however, that in 1495, partly because of the deterioration of the stone—which made any inscription illegible—common tradition had transformed it into the artist's tomb. We may therefore conclude that the epitaph revealed for the first time by Van Vaernewijck in 1568 is not sufficient evidence of Hubrecht's existence.

In the same context let us examine the famous four lines inscribed upon the lower edge of the polyptych's two outer shutters:

> *Ubertus Eyck maior quo nemo repertus*
> *incepit pondusq(ue) Johannes arte secundus*
> *. . . iodoci vyd prece fretus*
> *versu sexta mai vos collocat acta tueri*

This may be translated:

"The painter Hubert Van Eyck, greater than whom there is none to be found, commenced (this picture); this major work was, at the request and expense of Jodoc Vydt, completed by his brother John, who in art comes next after him. Today May 6 (1432), he invites you with this verse to admire the finished work."

The first part of the third line, partially erased, has been the subject of different translations; in the majority of cases the words *frater perfecit*, or something like it, have been deciphered, enabling one to get the general meaning of the phrase. It is astonishing to find the famous court painter of the Duchy of Burgundy admitting—on the very body of his masterpiece—that he is inferior to his brother Hubrecht, a man whom art historians have never been able to trace. The fact is that the inscription's authenticity is suspect, not least because of the clumsy writing. During the polyptych's restoration, in 1950–1 at the Laboratoire Central des Musées de Belgique, the various layers of paint and color upon the panels and the original frames of the shutters were closely examined. The experts were struck by the difference between the gold-leaf enveloping the frames of the inner panels and the silver-leaf around the frame of the outer shutters, on which the previous verse is inscribed. The silver-leaf is applied in two superimposed layers of which the lower layer has deteriorated in an irregular fashion and is similar in appearance to the preparatory layer under the gold-leaf of the inner panels. This leads one to conclude that at some unestablished date the whole original surface of the outer frames disappeared and was later entirely restored. It follows that chemical analysis carried out in the laboratory has cast doubts on the authenticity of the four lines of verse, though without proving that they are apocryphal. Moreover, other means of investigation—such as the detailed examination of the substance underneath the inscription—confirm such doubts.

The last line of verse is in fact a chronogram; that is, if the Roman-numeral letters in it are added, they give the date (1432) on which the altarpiece was placed inside the chapel. A specialist in these matters, James Hilton (1882–5), was suspicious *a priori* of all chronograms before 1450 and, indeed, even of those before about 1500. In this particular case he believed the chronogram in question to have been compiled in or about 1600. His opinion coincides with the date on which the inscription was first mentioned in literary sources, that is, between 1616 and 1621, by Christopher van Huerne. None of the visitors who admired the masterpieces in the Cathedral of St John (now St Bavon) at Ghent between 1432 and 1568, mentioned the inscription. The famous four lines were therefore apparently unknown in 1568.

The fact that these texts—the epitaph and the verse—were quoted so late by literary sources does not help confirm their authenticity and actually favors the theory of arbitrary and deliberate falsification. But, whether this was accidental or deliberate, everything points to the fact that for a long time no one believed the evidence. From 1608, the epitaph was not included in the list compiled by that scrupulous collector of epigraphs, the Dutch writer, Franc Sweertius. It can also be assumed that, a short time after its appearance the verse was covered by a layer of green paint which was removed in Berlin in 1823. The literary sources of the seventeenth century no longer quote the lines. Perhaps the authorities whose duty it was to preserve the altarpiece realized that they had made a mistake, either through irresponsibility or premeditation. One cannot otherwise explain the disappearance—in such a short time—of both epitaph and verse—supposed to be the two fundamental documents in support of Hubert.

Despite all these arguments, should one still wish to claim that Hubrecht Van Eyck lived and painted—if only because tradition says so—not even this hypothesis can survive in the face of a serious enquiry. Until the beginning of the sixteenth century, writers referred unanimously only to Jan, whom they generally called Jean de Bruges or Johannes Gallicus. He was praised by Ciriaco de' Pizzicolli of Ancona (1454), Bartolomeo Facio (1454), Antonio

Averulino, also known as *Il Filarete* (1464), Giovanni Santi (1485) and others. For over half a century all conceivable merits were attributed only to Jan. This is testified in writing by Jean Lemaire de Belges (1504), Albrecht Dürer (1521), Giorgio Vasari (1550 and 1568), Lambert Lombard (1565) and even Marcus van Vaernewijck (1568). But in 1517 the first doubts were expressed about the polyptych's authorship. In that year Cardinal Louis of Aragon began an important tour of western and central Europe; he was accompanied by his secretary, Antonio de Beatis, Canon of Melfi. After they had dutifully inspected the *Adoration of the Sacred Lamb* in Ghent, the secretary wrote: "The Canons of St John's church have told us that this altarpiece was painted a hundred years ago by a master of German extraction called Robert. As he died before finishing it, the work was completed by his brother who, like him, was a great painter." The casualness and lack of factual information in this passage are typical of the way in which legends are gradually created around those great historical figures for whom people have a particular veneration. The idea of an elder brother and collaborator of Jan gradually became popular belief. Lucas de Heere was the first, in 1565, to become a spokesman for the myth, which he did in an Ode expressly written in praise of the polyptych. The Ode reveals a juxtaposition of two traditions: first, in the longer and older part of the poem, he recognized and praised only Jan, but in the second and more recently written part he introduced the idea of a brother, Hubrecht. The two theories of Lucas de Heere were to reappear later in the writings of various authors, such as Lodovico Guicciardini (1567), Giorgio Vasari (1568), Marcus van Vaernewijck (1568), Dominicus Lampsonius (1572), Carel van Mander (1604) and Pieter Opmeer (1611).

What is one to conclude? Jan Van Eyck left many signed and dated works: Hubrecht none. Several written and official records of his time allow us to follow the course of Jan's life and career from 1422 to 1441: we have shown on the other hand what little importance can be attributed to the documents, the epitaph and the verse which are alleged to be proof of Hubrecht's existence. Apart from the mysterious Robert mentioned by De Beatis, Hubrecht's name appears nowhere before 1565, when Lucas de Heere first praises it in his Ode. One may indeed also suspect De Herre of having written, between 1565 and 1568, the apocryphal epitaph. It is possible that some vague recollection of Jan's real brother Lambrecht Van Eyck, who was a mediocre painter, was the origin of all the more or less improbable inventions about Hubrecht. The Ghent archives recorded, on September 18, 1426, the death of one *Hubrecht Van Heycke*; this may have been enough for popular legend to crystallize and become fact. We do know that the surviving documents are not sufficient proof of the actual existence of a painter called Hubrecht Van Eyck, an elder brother of Jan and the better artist of the two. Furthermore, the recent and thorough technical examination carried out by the Laboratoire Central des Musées de Belgique has failed to reveal the slightest trace of the participation of another hand—Hubrecht's—in the *Adoration of the Sacred Lamb* altarpiece. P. Coremans, of the Laboratoire, reported: "We have closely examined the painting, both on the surface and below, in order to discover in it the hand of a second great master, but we have failed to do so." This coincides, incidentally, with the historical and stylistic theories formulated by Karl Voll (1900), Frederik Lyna (1931), Emile Renders (1933) and Jacques Lavalleye (1943).

In the face of this mass of negative evidence there is no

reason to dwell any longer on the question of Hubrecht; our study of Jan's works can now be continued with greater ease and on more solid foundations.

The *Adoration of the Sacred Lamb* (plates 7–72) in Ghent's St Bavon Cathedral is the *chef d'œuvre* of Jan Van Eyck. In this work and for the first time, he was able to show the full measure of his superb qualities. In the first place the enormous size of the polyptych, larger than any previous easel painting by Van Eyck, is the exception of the whole of the fifteenth century. For this reason the assembly of no less than twenty panels was believed to have been commissioned by some great lord for the high altar of a cathedral. As the name of Philip the Good was never mentioned in connexion with this work, some assumed that Jan may have begun it at the request of the Prince of Bavaria, Count of Holland, whom he served between 1422 and 1425. This is mere speculation, unsupported by documentary evidence, except perhaps for the fact that the tower of Utrecht's Cathedral is very clearly visible in the background of the great lower-center panel portraying the actual *Adoration* (plates 8 and 9). On the other hand, the laboratory examination carried out in Belgium, has definitely proved that the tower was not part of the original layer of paint, but was added later, probably in the course of the somewhat radical restorations by Lancelot Blondeel in 1550 and especially by Jan Van Scorel, then Canon of Utrecht. However, even if it is reasonable to assume that the polyptych was not originally commissioned by the donors portrayed upon the outer shutters, one should conclude that it was completed at their request, and that they ultimately paid for the work. Münzer (1495) and other writers after him, reported that the patrons were indeed so pleased with the finished work that they paid Van Eyck an additional sum of six hundred *kronen*, or

16

groats. This would not be at all surprising on the part of such solid patricians as Joos Vijdt, Lord of Pamel, and his wife Isabelle Borluut: both were rich and their wealth accrued from 1425 to 1433-4, when Joos became Mayor of the City of Ghent. As they had no children, the Vijdts could afford princely gestures, such as the founding of a hospital at Beveren-Waas. One can accept, therefore, that even though their family chapel in St Baron Cathedral was a small one, they commissioned for it a work of art commensurate with their enormous fortune.

As with most problems concerning Jan Van Eyck's artistic production, there have been heated arguments about the exact definition of the *Adoration*'s subject. Many of the proposed explanations should, in my opinion, be discarded because they either go back to incredibly remote sources, or else appear unnecessarily complicated. Undoubtedly the subject of such a work was meant to be understood by all religious people, and for this reason it is generally believed that the theme of the painting was the Redemption. It is possible that Jan Van Eyck drew his inspiration partially from the Apocalypse (VII, 9), but it is also true that in his painting he recalled, very simply and effectively, the prelude to Christ's Redemption and the most tangible effects of that event. In the choice of subjects for the outer part of the shutters, Van Eyck showed himself a daring innovator, for he planned to establish—and did—a close and logical relationship between the outer and inner figures of the polyptych. This, when closed (plate 7), foretells the Redeemer's arrival by showing, in the upper lunettes, the prophets Zechariah and Micah, with the Erythraean and Cumaean Sibyls: as in the Morality Plays of the Middle Ages, these figures intervene in the spectacle's prologue; the influence of the theater of Van Eyck's day—which was to leave a deep impression on all Flemish painting of the fifteenth century—is particularly evident in this case. Like the title of a book, the four scrolls depicted upon the upper part of the shutters announce the two fundamental thoughts governing the open polyptych: "The Messiah will come and He will be King."

The full breadth of the exterior middle zone—still with the shutters closed—portrays the *Annunciation*: here the Angel Gabriel salutes the Virgin (plates 56 and 57). Iconographically, this is the first episode of Christ's redeeming mission. The artist's intense objectivity transforms Mary's room in Nazareth into a typical Flemish interior of the fifteenth century (plates 64 and 65): the eye is caught by the oak ceiling with its powerful rafters; by the trefoliated *oculus* beneath which a bronze vessel is suspended over a basin with a long towel hanging at its side; other objects of everyday use are seen in a niche; from the two-light window looking out on to the animated city streets below sunshine pours into the room.

Van Eyck completed the outer shutters' decorations by painting, in the lower zone, four identical niches with the *Donors* (plate 67) and two *St Johns* inside them (plate 66). The Saints have the stony appearance of statues, obviously in order to stress the contrast between them and the two human figures, represented kneeling with their hands joined in prayer. Joos Vijdt and Isabelle Borluut are certainly the most interesting figures on the shutters because of their fantastic plasticity, the psychological subtlety of their expressions, the choice, intimate sobriety of their coloring. These two figures are the only parts of the closed polyptych painted entirely in color and therefore contrast even more with the *chiaroscuro* (black and white) of John the Baptist—to whom the Cathedral was then dedicated—and John the Evangelist, author of the Apocalypse. The other figures on the shutters are also painted in *chiaroscuro*, touched here and there with color.

Having had this first encounter with Van Eyck's technique, when confronted with the open altarpiece one is none the less again astonished by the light, the chromatic splendor, the multitude of details and simultaneously the intensity of religious feeling. The whole lower zone (plates 32–33, 46 and 47) depicts a truly enchanting vision of the Garden of Eden. In a beautiful setting of sloping hills we see, in the foreground, a meadow sprinkled with every variety of flower; higher up the slope in the middle-distance are, on each side, flowering plants, shrubs and trees, all typical of the southern as well as the northern countries. These show that Van Eyck wanted to portray a symbolic picture of the ideal residence of the chosen few, rather than a particular aspect of the real world. Next to cypresses, pines, orange-trees, palms, pomegranates, fig-trees, and vines are maples, beeches, a rosebush, cherry-tree, and a gooseberry-bush. Finally, beyond the sinuous skyline of the hills, the roofs and towers of "God's City", the "Heavenly Jerusalem", are seen against the hazy background of distant mountains and a serene sky. At the center of the masterly composition the Mystical Lamb, as described by St John, stands on the altar, and from its spotless breast a stream of blood flows into a golden chalice. Angels kneel all around, the two in front of the altar swinging thuribles. In the center foreground is a fountain with a bronze column in the middle surmounted by a golden angel. Round the head of the stone basin an inscription explains that this is the Fountain of Life, symbol of the Redemption. Pearls, rubies and diamonds cover the bed of the little brook formed by water falling in tiny jets upon the earth. Groups of figures converge from all directions toward the twin symbols of the Lamb and the

Fountain, in accordance with Christ's words: "And when I shall have been removed from this earth I shall draw all men unto me." In the middle-distance, on the left, the Confessors and Martyrs advance, wearing vestments of blue and gold brocade; on the right are the Martyred Virgins in multi-colored robes.

On the left-hand panels (plate 46) two groups of horse-men proceed towards the altar: these are the *Just Judges*, richly clad in velvet and furs, and preceded by the *Knights of Christ*. In the center panel (plates 32 and 33), on the left, the Prophets kneeling in the foreground are followed by a group of robe-clad figures, some of whom are of Oriental origin. In all probability they are the Patriarchs, Poets and Philosophers of antiquity who believed in the Messiah's advent; to the right, behind the kneeling Apostles in their grayish-violet cloaks, stand three Popes, seven Bishops and Abbots and other Church Dignitaries, clad in magnificent vestments. Much rougher and harsher in appearance are the Hermits and Pilgrims, painted in gray and brown tones on the right-hand panel (plate 47). The austerity of these figures is only partially relieved by the presence of two women, St Mary Magdalene and St Mary of Egypt, who follow the Hermits from behind some rocks. All the groups in the lower zone are illuminated by the golden rays from the Holy Dove, poised high over the altar in a glory of rainbow colors.

Jan Van Eyck made a definite distinction between the upper and lower zones of the open polyptych by giving monumental dimensions to the figures of the upper part, representing the Celestial Paradise. His choice of charac-ters appears to have been inspired not only by the Apocalypse but also by the Mass of All Saints Day. At the two far ends (plate 27) the first man and woman are shown: their presence means that the human race, though fallen, has regained the right to eternal salvation. The nakedness of the two figures is stressed to the point of near crudity, establishing beyond all doubt that the artist used live models—further proof of his love of objective precision: the silvery reflections created here and there by light falling on the hairs of a figure's legs are due to the artist's method of scraping the surface with a dry, pointed instrument, very delicately, so that in these places the brilliant white preparatory substance under the paint is exposed to the light. One can easily understand how these nudes, the earliest in Flemish art, surprised Van Eyck's contemporaries—so much so that for a long time the polyptych was commonly described as the "picture of Adam and Eve". Above the founders of the human race two small *chiaroscuri* (plate 26) hint discreetly at their sinful descendants, but Abel's sacrifice of the Lamb is also a symbol of the Eucharist, and Cain's murderous deed is a pre-figuration of the death of Christ.

Nearer the center (plates 20 and 21) we find the *Angels playing and singing*, whose faces and robes have unfortunately been repainted, with the exception of the magnificent mantle of black-and-gold brocade worn by the organ player. Van Eyck achieved an almost tangible quality in the material substance of the harp, the five-stringed viol, the organ and the lectern.

The polyptych's general view is dominated by the three majestically enthroned figures of God (plate 10), the Virgin (plate 14), and John the Baptist (plate 15). The latter, wearing a moss-green mantle over a brown camel-hair robe, resembles an austere anchorite, but this severity is mitigated by the expression on his face, conscious of his great mission. The Virgin, clothed in a blue dress and billowing blue cloak, suggests a feeling of mysticism utterly devoid of preciosity. She appears as the Queen not only of Heaven but also of purity, love and humility; her gold crown is adorned not only with precious jewels and pearls, but with lilies and roses from the fields. Art historians and theologians have discussed at some length the central figure of the altarpiece. Is it God the Father or God the Son? Both are acceptable. However, assuming that the figure has come down to us as Van Eyck originally painted it, one may perhaps interpret it as a joint symbol of the first two persons of the union of the Holy Trinity.

In order to achieve a clear impression of the polyptych's appearance in its entirety, we should ask ourselves whether the altarpiece did in fact have beneath it a predella on which Jan Van Eyck had painted a picture of Hell. This was first stated by Marcus van Vaernewijck (1568) and repeated by Carel van Mander (1604) and other historians. What should be think? Van Vaernewijck's assertion seems doubtful, not only because it was made so late and was the only one of its kind before 1600, but also because—as he admits—the predella had disappeared in his own time. Furthermore, Michel Coxcie, who made a copy of the altarpiece for Philip II in 1559, did not reproduce the predella. In the absence of more positive evidence doubt must remain, except for this one qualification: if there ever was a predella below the *Adoration of the Sacred Lamb* it is much more likely to have portrayed not Hell but Purgatory—a subject considerably more in tune with the dominating concept of the polyptych.

One of Van Eyck's greatest merits is the fact that he set the pattern for over a century for the whole of Flemish art. To this day we are dazzled by the splendor of his works and those of his followers. It is as if their pictures concealed a source of light beneath the paint. This is indirectly true, and one of Van Eyck's greatest achievements. Van Eyck's technique resulted, of course, from the work of some of his great predecessors between the fourteenth and fifteenth centuries, but he was the first to practise it in an exemplary manner. Its fundamental principles have been recently analyzed, after a very close study of his pictures, at the Laboratoire Central in Brussels.

The main support of the picture always consisted of one or more panels of oak, upon which was spread a very thin layer of chalk and animal glue. The first and foremost function of this white preparation was to smooth and even out the wooden surface. It also reflected any solar or artificial light cast upon the painting; light easily penetrated the various coatings of color, which were generally transparent. I should like to stress this point: Van Eyck made constant use of the *velatura* method, that is, a series of superimposed layers incorporating the colored substances in one glossy medium. The percentage of chromatic pigments used was calculated beforehand in order to avoid opaqueness. In contrast with the Italian primitives and their contemporaries abroad who followed the distemper technique, Van Eyck employed as a medium a form of siccative oil, possibly oil diluted with volatile turpentine. One can understand, therefore, why Vasari (1550) and Marcus van Vaernewijck (1568) called Jan the inventor of oil-painting—though in my opinion this is too sweeping a statement. It is true that Guicciardini (1567), Vasari (1568), Locrius (1616) and others, claim that Van Eyck had perfected his method as early as 1410, but it is far more reasonable to assume that his predecessors had already experimented with mixtures based upon siccative oil. This was believed by writers as early as Aubertus Miraeus (1608) and Emmanuel Sueyro (1624). My point may well be soon confirmed by scientific analysis in different countries.

Van Eyck's palette consisted of four fundamental colors: green, red, blue and white, to which derivations may be added such as pink, mauve, purple, violet, brown, gray, etc. He preferred warm tonalities; red, orange and yellow. All these colors were laid on as *velature*, the opaqueness and number of each being directly proportionate to the depth of the shadow he wished to obtain. It is indeed remarkable that an artist should paint the whole background of his picture—the landscape, for instance—before working on the figures and objects in the foreground.

But any technique is important only as an instrument subservient to an artistic concept. Van Eyck's technique had to be a revolutionary one because his representational taste had very little in common with that of his predecessors. Only in his art, in fact, do we find the modern concept of easel-painting, in other words, an apparently three-dimensional presentation of the visual world with all the consequences that implies. His departure from tradition is difficult to appreciate nowadays. Van Eyck was bold enough to renounce totally not only the temptations of late-Gothic decorative linearism, but also the flat golden backgrounds which deprived the works of Franco-Flemish painters and miniaturists of all depth. He replaced these with scenes, more or less remote, of landscape and interiors. Apart from the Sienese School of the fourteenth century, Pol, Hennequin and Herman of Limburg had undoubtedly made some remarkable experiments in this direction with their beautiful miniatures in the *Très riches Heures de Jean, duc de Berry* (Chantilly, 1409–16), but these do not diminish Van Eyck's masterly achievements. Indeed, one can say that he applied on a huge scale both linear and aerial perspective, that is to say, the perspective of lines and of colors.

Naturally Van Eyck suffered from initial doubts. In the inner lower zone of the *Adoration of the Sacred Lamb*, for instance, the groups are too crowded, and the artist avails himself of little mounds, employed as theatrical wings, in order to avoid the complicated problems of gradual perspective—the mastery of which he was to acquire only later. But apart from this, we can almost feel the sensations of space and open-air and the figures moving freely in the landscape. And how many discoveries there are to be made in following, along and below the skyline, the subtle passages from mountains to plains, rolling hills and woods! If one stops to think that, dimensionally speaking, the Ghent polyptych measures up to about twenty pictures of its time, one cannot but marvel at Van Eyck's sure touch in creating such a varied composition and, at the same time, in spite of the tremendous complexity of its theme, in achieving such a firm construction.

But Van Eyck could not introduce a third dimension in painting, that is to say depth, without transforming the whole concept of a picture accordingly. The characters of the cast could no longer be a series of figures, cut out and placed in profile against a flat surface. They had to be persons, endowed with a more obvious plastic value, and whose proportions must be far greater than those in miniatures. In the *Adoration of the Sacred Lamb* Van Eyck had already adopted for all his figures, but especially for the three central characters of the upper zone, a scale which can well be described as monumental. One is surprised at the volumes of their vestments and at the natural, free-flowing depth of their drapery. It is true that while he was still influenced by the thirteenth-century taste, Van Eyck's drapery appeared superficial and rather too rounded, but it later became more clear-cut and angular: this development is clearly seen in the Ghent polyptych which was painted over a number of years. Here we are confronted with one of Jan Van Eyck's dominating qualities, a quality which was, furthermore, to become a feature of the whole of Flemish art: his incomparable feeling for the material aspect of each and every object that he painted. He was most anxious to render faithfully even the most insignificant details. Through the windows of the *Annunciation*, on the outer part of the polyptych, one can see not only other houses in detail, but even the passers-by, their clothes, their shadows. Each hair of Eve's head is clearly distinguishable; pearls, precious stones, breast-plates, flesh, rocks and plants, brocades and furs—all give the illusion of reality. The photographic enlargements of the polyptych's single parts show what loving and painstaking care Van Eyck could put into depicting the smallest reflection of the visible world.

What makes Van Eyck's technical and formal qualities so outstanding is, moreover, the spiritual message which he conveys through them. His subjects are still religious in essence, and treated with an exemplary religious feeling. Indeed, one may go so far as to say that his secret lies in a rare and balanced synthesis of naturalistic objectivity and mystical inspiration. In spite of the more human and earthly aspect of his saints, his angels and their surroundings, whoever gazes upon them cannot but feel deeply moved and inspired. In order to communicate to others that ancient faith which he felt in absolute sincerity and simplicity, Van Eyck chose to employ the elements offered him by the visible world. That is why that aura of unreality which is common to all mystical representations is not at first apparent in his works—his figures and objects have such an everyday appearance. The most brilliant musician at the court of Philip the Good, Guillaume Dufay, composed religious music and even polyphonic Masses, whose melodies were taken from earlier secular songs. This was in no way harmful to the intensity of faith expressed in his compositions. The same relationship could be traced between the immediate realism of Van Eyck's details and the religious inspiration behind his paintings.

This great inspiration, and the formal language of Van Eyck, both so well exemplified in the *Adoration of the Sacred Lamb*, can also be detected, though less obviously in some of his earlier works. The two New York panels—the attributions of which are controversial—showing the *Crucifixion* and *The Last Judgement* (plate 136), prove that the artist, when still young and artistically not fully developed, was content with painting against a flat background or giving his picture an uphill, rather indefinite, perspective. The Berlin *Crucifixion* (plate 41)—equally controversial —already shows a greater freedom from the late-Gothic manner of traditional miniaturists; Van Eyck's pictorial language appears more clearly and firmly formulated. His flora seems, though confusedly, to forecast that of the Ghent altarpiece. The exasperated painful expression of the figures in the *Crucifixion* still reflects the general tendencies of non-Italian painting at the beginning of the fifteenth century. The *Stigmatization of St Francis*, now in Philadelphia (plate 4), can well stand comparison with the *Adoration of the Sacred Lamb* at Ghent: its technique is both subtle and precise and its formal plasticity most lively and a religious serenity shines through the picture. The same cannot be said of Berlin's *Madonna in a Church* (plate 1) which, though rich in finely executed details and gentle shades of color, still appears as a work of transition from the New York diptych—if the authorship be accepted—to Van Eyck's first great masterpieces.

All the scenes painted by Van Eyck after the Ghent altar-piece are connected with the Virgin's iconographic cycle, with the exception of a rather late drawing of *St Barbara* (plate 122) at Antwerp. The artist's hand, at once soft and incisive, portrayed in the middle-distance a massive tower in the course of construction, isolated against a wide landscape. Van Eyck must have liked this unfinished work, for though it was probably a preparatory drawing for a picture, he set it within a beautiful frame recalling a marble frieze. Most of his original frames, in fact, suggest marble or stone.

In the series of themes centered on the Virgin, Van Eyck painted two *Annunciations*. The two Lugano organ-shutters (plates 104 and 105) show the Angel Gabriel and Mary standing upon two pedestals, like stone statues. The figures immediately recall those of the *Annunciation* on the outer part of the Ghent polyptych, as well as—for their sculptoral character—the two St Johns. In the Lugano figures, how-ever, Van Eyck places his two painted statues of white stone against a background imitating polished black marble. This device enables him to reproduce, partially at least, the gray "smoked" reflections of his two pieces of "sculpture".

The Washington *Annunciation* (plate 81) is an entirely different work. The event takes place in the choir of an unusual three-aisled Romanesque church with a flat ceiling. The words of the angelic salutation are inscribed in the same way as those in the similar scene on the Ghent altarpiece. The eye of the observer is especially caught by Gabriel's beautiful cape of dark red and gold worn over a tunic of green-and-gold velvet brocade, and by the magnificent floor of storied panels showing scenes from the lives of Sampson and David.

All the remaining religious subjects painted by Van Eyck

portray exclusively the Virgin and Child. In more than one case the picture shows only the two figures in an idealized scene of intimacy and devotion. In this connexion it is important to mention the Antwerp masterpiece, *The Virgin at the Fountain* (plate 124), in which two angels are seen holding up a beautiful "cloth of honor", of red-and-gold brocaded damask, behind the Virgin, who stands by a metal fountain with four jets. In the background, on each side of the cloth, is a low bank faced with masonry and covered with fine grass and flowering plants, and a thick hedge of purple roses and lilies. Van Eyck's signature upon the frame is superfluous, for his simple faith, his refined composition, his loving attention to detail throughout the work are typical of him. Furthermore, the Virgin is typical of the artist's concept: clad in fifteenth-century dress, round-headed with rather a full face, a high forehead and silken blonde hair, and hands that are small and slender.

The same type of Virgin appears in the *Lucca Madonna* (plate 102), now at Frankfurt. Attired in an ample crimson mantle, she is seated inside a small room on an oak throne under a velvet canopy, giving the Child her breast. A barely visible window on the left enables the artist to graduate his shades *ad infinitum*; the result is pure and sublime poetry. The *Ince Hall Madonna* at Melbourne (plate 79), unfortunately in poor condition, seems to be a second version of the Frankfurt masterpiece.

The three main representations of the Virgin painted by Van Eyck portray Saints and donors next to the sacred figures. In the *Madonna Triptych* (Dresden), representing the Virgin and Child with SS Catherine and Michael and the Donor (plates 96 and 97), Mary and Jesus occupy the central panel. The Virgin is seen enthroned under a monumental canopy in the choir of a church similar to the one in the

Washington *Annunciation*. Everything here is richly adorned, multi-coloured floor, carpets and brocades, Romanesque capitals, statues and glass windows. The lesser naves are continued upon the shutters: at right a regal St Catherine, patroness of the learned, is depicted standing and reading a book; at left, St Michael, in splendid armor, protects the kneeling donor. Here St Michael is the immediate prototype of St George worshipping the *Virgin with Canon van der Paele* at Bruges (plate 111). The triptych's exterior depicts, as usual, the *Annunciation* in *chiaroscuro* (plate 100). The picture's general appearance is most reminiscent of the Lugano shutters.

The *Virgin with Chancellor Rolin*, at the Louvre (plate 106), is one of the greatest expressions not only of Van Eyck's but of the whole of Flemish art. Its dimensions are neither too large nor too small, but ideally suited to easel-painting, and its composition is a delicate balance of grandeur and detail of selectivity. Van Eyck's colors attain a degree of refinement eminently suited to the highest dignitary in Philip the Good's court. The mighty Chancellor is seen wearing a brocade mantle; although he kneels with joined hands before the Child his hard inflexible eyes still reflect all his authority. Opposite him, the monumental Madonna holding the Child appears modest and even shy; an angel holds above her head the most beautiful bejeweled crown "ever fashioned by the hands of a painter"; certainly it is the most splendid crown ever painted by Van Eyck. In the background an elegant treble-arched arcade opens on to a garden of flowering plants, beyond which is a raised terrace with peacocks and figures of men. Farther away still is a landscape recalling Burgundy, or the Meuse countryside, intersected by a broad river. More than one scholar has tried to identify the town seen through the arches, but until now no theory has been accepted. The almost incredible love for detail brought by Van Eyck to this work—note the comings-and-goings of the townsmen and the structure of the buildings—surpasses even the *tour de force* of the Ghent altarpiece.

Another culminating point in Van Eyck's painting of religious subjects is the *Virgin with Canon van der Paele* at Bruges (plate 111), which is fortunately still in excellent condition. This picture's dimensions are much greater than those of the previous painting. The seated Virgin recalls those of Frankfurt and Dresden but her general appearance is more monumental. The portrayal donor makes what is possibly the finest portrait in Flemish art of the fifteenth century, especially in the face, which conveys a striking feeling of physical and moral integrity. He kneels opposite St Donatian who is robed in a splendid cope of blue-and-gold velvet brocade, and is protected by his name-saint, St George, who stands behind him clad in a splendid suit of armor. The powerful impression of tangible and visual reality created by each detail of this painting is heightened when one examines the carpet leading up to the throne. In spite of the picture's realism and the total absence of any attempt at idealization, the religious character of this first Flemish "Sacred Conversation" is essentially respected. The objectivity and plausibility of the composition's details do not detract in the slightest from the faith that it engenders. This, indeed, is the apex of all of Van Eyck's efforts and experiments.

A close study of the master's religious works reveals very clearly that he was also an exceptionally gifted portrait painter. Although, in this particular field especially, he was a renovator, he quickly achieved such perfection that one may dismiss any thought of development. Less than ten years separate the *Virgin with Canon van der Paele* from Van Eyck's first portrait, that of *Cardinal Albergati* (plate 73). As was his habit, he painted the sitter to the waist in three-quarter profile with the head turned to the right. The dark, neutral background brings out the Cardinal's head. The preparatory drawing, kept in Dresden, shows a number of notes in Van Eyck's hand, relating to the color of each detail of the face. One is immediately struck by the master's craftsmanship, technical assurance and accuracy blended with economy. In fact, it is difficult not to prefer to the painting the exquisite drawing in silver-point on a white ground, for the painting, completed in the Cardinal's absence, seems somehow less alive and direct.

This difficulty does not recur in Van Eyck's other portraits, some of which depict sitters altogether unknown, such as the *Portrait of a young man* (plate 75), and the *Man in a turban* (plate 77), both in London's National Gallery, the *Portrait of a goldsmith* in Rumania and the donor of the *Madonna Triptych* in Dresden; nor can one overlook certain figures of saints which have all the appearance of portraits, as in the case, for instance, of the *Stigmatization of St Francis* in Philadelphia, looking at which one is tempted to think of a donor's portrait. But of all these anonymous figures the most outstanding is certainly the *Man in a turban* because of the economic representation of each facial feature, their plastic quality, the vitality of the eyes and the enigmatic quality surrounding the whole figure.

Not all of Jan's sitters, however, are unknown to us. Among his more orthodox works one should mention the Berlin portrait of *Giovanni Arnolfini* (plate 86), Vienna's portrait of *Jan De Leeuw* (plate 120), and especially the portrait of *Baldovino de Lannoy*, also in Berlin (plate 121). These three pictures are sufficient proof that Van Eyck's fundamental objectivity did not tolerate the slightest concession to adulation. The only female portrait that he painted, that of his wife, *Margharita Van Eyck* (plate 126), is composed along the lines of his habitual schemes. The artist's motto, "As I can", would seem in this case to be not so much an expression of modesty as a preventive self-defence against all possible criticism on the part of the woman whose character and features he had immortalized with such merciless accuracy. But to our eyes, the portrait remains an unforgettable masterpiece.

Only once did Jan Van Eyck depart from his scheme and that was when he painted his only double portrait, the *Marriage of Giovanni Arnolfini and Giovanni Cenami* (London, National Gallery, plate 87). The two are seen standing in their bedroom, a Flemish interior. One is immediately struck by the pure beauty of the coloring and particularly by the woman's light-green dress. After that the eye is arrested by the many objects in the room, but their material appearance, reproduced with the artist's usual accuracy, does not diminish the picture's symbolic significance. The subtle, discreet interplay of light and shadow creates an atmosphere of delicate and serene intimacy. As in the case of the *Lucca Madonna*, and indeed here more successfully, Van Eyck availed himself of lateral daylight.

It would hardly be fair, in this brief essay on Van Eyck's portrait painting, not to mention the donors portrayed in his principal sacred works: Joos Vijdt and Isabelle Borluut (Ghent), Chancellor Rolin (Paris) and Canon van der Paele (Bruges). Though once again perfectly faithful in their physical and moral characteristics, these four portraits are all animated by an intense religious feeling that one would seek in vain in Van Eyck's individual portraits.

Once one has considered Van Eyck's astonishing works

in all their aspects, one cannot but admire the authority with which he established the fundamental pattern of the whole of Flemish painting in the fifteenth century. Only one of his pupils is known, Peter Christus. Yet the impression remains that most artists working in Bruges at the time drew from him some vital element of one kind or another. All followed his example, even some of the great painters who came after him—Roger Van der Weyden, Hugo Van der Goes, Dirck Bouts and Memling.

The international character of Philip the Good's court, with people always coming and going, Van Eyck's many journeys, and the fact that his works were sent to all countries in Europe, explain how his influence soon spread abroad. In France it conditioned the activities of the "Master of the Aix *Annunciation*", of Simon Marmion, of Nicolas Froment; in Italy Antonello da Messina showed his respect by assimilating some of Jan's technical and formal contributions. But the strongest effect outside Flanders was felt in the Iberian Peninsula: Nuño Gonçalves in Portugal, Pedro Berruguete, Jacomart Baço and Luis Dalmau in Spain all drew great inspiration from the works of "the illustrious Jan of Bruges".

BIOGRAPHICAL NOTES

1390 (*circa*). Birth of Jan Van Eyck in the Limburg-Meuse region (Maastricht or its immediate surroundings).

1422–5. Attached to the household of John of Bavaria, Count of Holland, at The Hague.

1425–6. Lives at Lille.

1425–41. Appointed Court-painter to Philip the Good, Duke of Burgundy.

1427, October 18. Is sent by Philip on a secret mission to the city of Tournai, where he is presented with the wine of honor.

1428–9. Is sent by Philip with an official delegation to the King of Portugal, to beg the hand of the Princess Isabella. Van Eyck paints her portrait.

1430, January 7. Is present at the marriage of Philip and Isabella at Sluus.

1431–41. Lives at Bruges.

1431–2. Draws and paints the portrait of *Cardinal Albergati*.

1432. Buys a house at Bruges and is visited by the city burgomaster and other members of the town-council. Paints his first signed picture, a *Portrait of a young man* (London, National Gallery). An apocryphal stanza would have it that the *Adoration of the Lamb*, completed by Jan, was unveiled on May 6, 1432.

1433. Philip the Good visits his home.

1434. Is married to Margherita (in April). Their first child is born in June and the Duke is god-father at the christening.

1439. Paints his last signed picture, a portrait of his wife (Bruges).

1441, July 9. Dies at Bruges and is later buried in the church of St Donatian which no longer exists.

1449. His daughter, Livina, enters the convent of St Agnes at Maaseik.

1454. Jan Van Eyck's art is praised for the first time by Ciriaco de' Pizzicolli, of Ancona.

PAINTINGS BY JAN VAN EYCK

Color Plate I–II

ADORATION OF THE SACRED LAMB, interior central panel (see plates 7–72).

Plate 1

MADONNA IN A CHURCH. *Oak, 32 × 14* (semi-circular at the top). Berlin, Kaiser Friedrich Museum.* Dated *circa* 1425 and generally attributed to Van Eyck. Previously (1855) in the F. Cacault Collection and later (1869) in the Nau Collection at Nantes. Purchased in 1874 at Aachen with the rest of the Guermondt Collection. One may well wonder if this was not the "small Virgin" recorded in 1649 in the inventory of the goods of Abraham Matthys at Antwerp. The disproportion between the Virgin and Child and the church's interior is intentional, for it stresses the great symbolic importance of the Mother of God. R. Laminaire (1950) suggests that Van Eyck modeled his church on the Cathedral of St Bavon at Ghent. There are copies of the picture in the Antwerp Museum—dated 1499—and in the Doria Gallery at Rome—early sixteenth century. Friedländer believes the latter to be by Jan Gossaert. (See also plates 2 and 3.)

Plate 2

MADONNA IN A CHURCH, detail: Madonna and Child.

Plate 3

MADONNA IN A CHURCH, detail of the right-hand background.

Plate 4

STIGMATIZATION OF ST FRANCIS. *Philadelphia, Pennsylvania Museum of Art, Collection of Mr John G. Johnson. Oak, 12·5 × 14·5. (The original measurements were reduced by 3·5 and 6·5 respectively by the restorer, Roger Fry.)* Dated about 1430. Generally attributed to Van Eyck, but the date is set at 1438–9 by Friedländer (1924) and Tolnay (1939). Purchased about 1830 at Lisbon by Lord Heytesbury, this picture has been in the Johnson Collection since 1890. It was mentioned in 1470 (February 10) in the will of Anselm Adornes, a Bruges resident of Genoese origin, whose son became Mayor of Bruges and who left to each of his two daughters, both nuns, a panel by Jan Van Eyck, representing St Francis. The second painting could be the very ancient copy in Turin's Galleria Sabauda which, however, does not appear to have been painted by Jan Van Eyck (see plate 156). In both pictures the monks Francis and Leo are wearing a brown and gray habit respectively, but the brown Franciscans, that is, the reformed order, did not found their first convent in the Netherlands until the end of the fifteenth century; before that time the habit worn in the Low Countries was

*All dimensions are given in centimeters.

37

gray. W. H. James Weale concluded from this that Van Eyck must have painted this work somewhere in the south of Europe, where the Franciscans had already adopted brown. One could equally assume from these facts that Van Eyck painted the panel on his return from a journey to the south. At the time of the artist's death Anselm Adornes, who was born in 1424, was only seventeen years old. We may deduce from this that the panel was commissioned from Van Eyck not by Anselm but by his father, Francesco (?) Adornes, nor can we reject the theory that Van Eyck portrayed this donor in his St Francis. The figure is iconographically too remote from the traditional image of the *Poverello di Assisi* ("Poor One of Assisi") not to make us think of a living model. Who could this model be if not, presumably, the donor? One is also struck by the absence of a tonsure on the Saint's head; the tonsure appears, however, in the Turin panel. (See also plates 5 and 6.)

Plate 5

STIGMATIZATION OF ST FRANCIS, detail: St Francis receiving the stigmata.

Plate 6

STIGMATIZATION OF ST FRANCIS, detail: Brother Leo sleeping.

THE ADORATION OF THE SACRED LAMB

Plates 7 to 72

Jan Van Eyck's greatest work is to be found in Ghent, in the Chapel of Joos Vijdt, inside the Cathedral of St Bavon. It is a great altarpiece consisting of twelve inner and eight outer panels. The dimensions of the whole polyptych equal 350 × 461. All the panels are of oak painted over with siccative oil. The eight outer panels are painted on the reverse of as many inner lateral panels, so that the oak panels constituting the polyptych proper are actually only twelve.

The theme is the Redemption. The work was probably executed between 1425 and 1432. On the lower edge of the outer shutters an apocryphal chronogram states that the altarpiece was begun by Hubrecht Van Eyck and completed by his brother Jan at the request of Joos Vijdt, and unveiled on May 6, 1432. (For this date and the existence of a Hubrecht Van Eyck see pages 10ff.) Let us recall here the main facts concerning the polyptych:

1433, November 20: Mentioned for the first time in official records.

1458, April 23: The whole altarpiece was the subject of a *tableau-vivant* in honor of Philip the Good's arrival at Ghent. A detailed description of the occasion in the *Kronijk van Vlaenderen* contains no mention of the predella upon which—as stated by M. van Vaernewijck—Jan was supposed to have painted in distemper a picture of Hell.

Before 1500: The altarpiece is partly defaced by cleaning.

1550, September 15: The work is rather freely restored by Jan Van Scorel and Lancelot Blondeel.

1566-9: To save it from iconoclasts the polyptych is hidden in the Cathedral's tower.

1569-78: It is returned to the Vijdt Chapel.

1578-84: The Calvinist leaders, wishing to give it to Queen Elisabeth through the good offices of the

Prince of Orange, had the altarpiece removed to the Town-House.

1584–5: It is placed in the Viglius Chapel, situated east of the Vijdt Chapel in the Cathedral.

1586: It is returned to the Vijdt Chapel.

1612: The polyptych is restored by Novelliers, of Brussels.

1640, June 1: The Cathedral's roof is destroyed by fire.

1663: The altarpiece is cleaned by Antoine Van den Heuvel.

1781, June 17: Inspected by the Emperor Joseph II.

1794: The polyptych's four central panels (*God, The Virgin, John the Baptist, The Adoration*) are taken to Paris and there exhibited. The shutter-panels are stored away somewhere in the Cathedral's precincts.

1816: The central panels are returned to Ghent. Except for those portraying Adam and Eve, the shutter-panels are sold to L. J. Nieuwenhuys of Brussels.

1817: The Solly Collection of Aachen purchases six shutter-panels.

1821: The Emperor Wilhelm III of Prussia purchases the whole Solly Collection and presents it to the Berlin Museum.

1822, September 11: The roofs of part of the Cathedral and of the Vijdt Chapel are burnt down. The whole central part of the altarpiece is seriously damaged.

1823: The original frames of the altarpiece shutters are cleaned in Berlin. The apocryphal lines are discovered.

1825–8: Restoration of the whole central part (four panels) by Lorent.

1858: Donselaer restores the panels portraying Adam and Eve.

1859: Donselaer restores the four panels of the central part.

1861, April 19: The panels portraying Adam and Eve are donated to the Belgian State and exhibited in the Brussels Museum. In Ghent only the central part (the four original panels) is exhibited. The shutters shown are taken from a copy by Michel Coxcie, made in 1559.

1894: In Berlin the six shutter-panels are sawn through, in order to exhibit simultaneously their outer and inner pictures.

1902, June 15–September 15: The Brussels Museum lends *Adam and Eve* to Bruges, for an exhibition.

1914–18: The polyptych's central part is hidden to protect it from possible war damage.

1920, November 6–1934, April 10: The Versailles treaty compels Germany to return the six shutter-panels. The polyptych is once again entirely visible in its original setting.

1923, May 10: *Adam and Eve* are exhibited in Paris, at the Musée de Jeu de Paume.

1934, night of April 10: the *Just Judges* and *John the Baptist* (exterior) are stolen.

1935, May 11: *John the Baptist* is recovered.

1935, November–1936, January: The portraits of Jodoc and Elisabeth Vijdt are shown in the Paris Exhibition of Flemish Primitives, at the Musée de l'Orangerie.

1937: Restoration of the *Adam and Eve* panels by Joseph Van der Veken.

1940–2: Because of the war the whole polyptych, from which the stolen panel of the *Just Judges* is still missing, is sent to the Castle of Pau.

1942, August–1945 May 8: The

polyptych is in German hands. They keep it first at Neuschwanstein, then in a salt-mine at Alt Aussee.

1945: The altarpiece is returned to Belgium (August 20), exhibited in Brussels (September 10–30) and restored to its original place. The original panel of the *Just Judges* is replaced by a copy painted by Joseph Van der Veken (1943–4), a capable restorer who, however, slightly altered the features of one figure to make him resemble King Leopold III.

1946: *Adam and Eve* are exhibited in Amsterdam (March 23–May 19) and at Rotterdam (May 25–June 16).

1950, October 13–1951, October 29: Excellent restoration carried out at the Laboratoire Central des Musées de Belgique in Brussels, under the supervision of Professor Paul Coremans and in collaboration with the restorer A. Philippot.

1951: After a brief exhibition in Brussels (October 30–November 19) the altarpiece is returned to the Vijdt Chapel in Ghent.

There are many copies of the polyptych:

A complete copy (panel) executed by Michel Coxcie in 1559 at the request of King Phillip II of Spain (Brussels Museum).

A complete copy (canvas) executed at the beginning of the seventeenth century by an anonymous artist for the Ghent Town Hall (Antwerp Museum).

A copy of the three central panels of the upper zone (*God, The Virgin,* and *John the Baptist*), executed in 1824 by Carl Friedrich Shultz (Berlin Museum).

A complete copy executed in 1845–6 by the De Pape brothers (lost).

A copy of *Adam and Eve* executed in 1861 by Victor Lagye (Ghent Cathedral).

A copy of the *Two Sibyls* executed in 1904 by Richard Böhnke (Berlin Museum).

A copy of the *Just Judges* executed in 1943–44 by Joseph Van der Veken and inserted in the body of the altarpiece to replace the original stolen panel.

Those art historians who believed in the collaboration between Hubrecht and Jan (Dvorak, Weale, Heidrich, Beenken, Panofsky, Tolnay, Hulin de Loo, Puyvelde, Mather and Baldass) have never succeeded in agreeing over the parts of the polyptych ascribable to one or the other Van Eyck. All the various parts, in fact, have been alternately attributed to Jan or Hubrecht, and this should be considered sufficient proof of the work's unity of style. The opinion expressed in this monograph, i.e. the attribution of the whole altarpiece to Jan, is accepted by Voll, Winkler, Friedländer and also by Ragghianti, who believes, however, the work to have been carried out at two different periods: first the *Adoration,* the *Knights of Christ* and the *Pilgrims,* and all the other parts at a later date.

Thanks to the courteous permission granted by the Laboratoire Central des Musées de Belgique, all the plates showing the entire polyptych —both closed and open—and most plates of the details, consist of photographs taken after the great restoration in 1950–1.

Plate 7
<small>GENERAL VIEW</small> (outside).

Plates 8–9
<small>GENERAL VIEW</small> (inside).

Plate 10

GOD, whole panel. *212·2 × 83·1*. Here one can only appreciate Van Eyck's mastery of composition, for the repaintings of the sixteenth and nineteenth centuries cover the whole original surface, or at least what is left of it. The inscriptions on this panel, and on the two on its right and left, have also been changed, but the original words are recorded in *Kronijk van Vlaenderen*. It is not certain if the artist wished to portray here God the Father or God the Son: the figure is probably a joint symbol of the first two of the union of the Holy Trinity. (See also plates 11–13 and 18.)

Plate 11

GOD, detail of the head.

Plate 12

GOD, detail of the hand.

Plate 13

GOD, detail of the tiara.

Plate 14

THE VIRGIN, whole panel. *168·7 × 74·9*. Except for the figure the whole panel was repainted about 1550. Before the 1950–1 restoration the Virgin's cloak was painted an unsightly green. Donselaer was said to have painted it over in ultramarine blue "to camouflage the cracks", and this modern pigment entirely concealed the drapery's original beauty. The removal of that superimposed coating is one of the most positive results of recent restoration. (See also plate 16.)

Plate 15

JOHN THE BAPTIST, whole panel. *Measurements 168·1 × 75·1* The figure, clad in a simple green mantle, has hardly been retouched. All the rest appears to have been repainted by Jan Van Scorel and Lancelot Blondeel (1550) in order to remedy damage caused by previous poor restoration. On the open book upon the Saint's knees one can read the word *Consolamini*, which opens Chapter 40 in the Book of Isaiah, where the prophet foretells the Baptist's mission. (See also plates 17 and 19.)

Plate 16

THE VIRGIN, detail of the face.

Plate 17

JOHN THE BAPTIST, detail of the face.

Plate 18

GOD, detail of the crown at the figure's feet.

Plate 19

JOHN THE BAPTIST, detail of the book.

Plate 20

ANGELS PLAYING AND SINGING, whole panel, on the left of *The Virgin. 164·5 × 71·5*. In examining this and the following panel one should keep in mind once again that, excepting the beautiful floors and the organ player's brocade mantle (plate 23), the two surfaces were entirely repainted at different periods. The white tiles on both floors are adorned with symbols painted in blue, such as the Lamb, the initials of Jesus and Mary, Alfa and Omega, and the abbreviation *AGLA*, consisting of the initials of Isaiah's prayer in Hebrew: "You, forever powerful, my God." (See the following plates up to plate 25.)

41

Plate 21

ANGELS PLAYING, whole panel, on the right of *The Virgin*. *164·1* × *72·9*. See comment to previous plate.

Plate 22

ANGELS SINGING, detail of three angels.

Plate 23

ANGELS PLAYING, detail of the organ player.

Plate 24

ANGELS SINGING, detail of singer's head.

Plate 25

ANGELS PLAYING, detail of organ player's stool and floor.

Plate 26

TWO BIBLICAL EPISODES above the panels of *Adam and Eve* (plate 27). In the first scene Cain and Abel are portrayed offering their sacrifice to God, whilst in the second one Cain is seen slaying Abel. See comment on page 21. The two small scenes, painted in *chiaroscuro* (black and white), give the impression of sculptured stone.

Plate 27

ADAM AND EVE, whole view of both panels. Dimensions (inclusive of the *Two Biblical Scenes* mentioned above): Adam—*219·9* × *37·1*; Eve—*213·3* × *32·3*. These two panels, as well as the small *chiaroscuri* above them, are in excellent condition, thereby allowing us to appreciate in full the master's magnifying-glass clarity of vision. The naked eye can easily detect an alteration in the lower part of Adam's legs. X-rays have shown that

their original position was exactly the same as that of Eve's limbs. Van Eyck himself was responsible for the alteration in order, surely, to avoid an excess of symmetry. Psychologically both figures appear fully conscious of their guilt, but Adam's contrition is obviously deeper and more keenly understood than that of his companion. (See also plates 28 to 31.)

Plate 28

ADAM, detail of the head.

Plate 29

EVE, detail of the head.

Plate 30

ADAM, detail of the face.

Plate 31

EVE, detail of the face.

Plates 32–33

THE ADORATION, whole central panel of the altarpiece. *137·7* × *243·3*. See comment pages 19ff. Before the 1950–1 restoration the panel clearly showed the more serious damage caused by fire in 1822: the burnt parts had been glued together and incompetently repainted, especially in the area between the altar, the Utrecht tower, and the *Virgins* group. All traces of this bad restoration have now disappeared, and the original planes of the vast Walloon lowlands are once again visible. The dove, too, before the restoration was surrounded by heavy gray clouds, which have now given place to the original semi-circular halo of rainbow-colored light. The Lamb, as visible today, was obviously repainted during the last century. The

42

altar frontal in red-and-gold brocade bears the legends: *Ecce Agnus Dei qui tollit pec(c)a(ta) mundi*, and *I H S (Iesus) Via, Veritas, vita*. Round the head of the octagonal basin another inscription appears, taken from the Apocalypse (xxii): *Hic est fons aque vite procedens de sede Dei*. Among the group of *Martyred Virgins*, right and in the middle-distance, one can identify SS Dorothy, Catherine, Barbara and Agnes. Below, among the great dignitaries of the Church, and one behind the other, are SS Stephen and Livin, patron of Ghent, (See also plates 34 to 45.)

Plate 34

THE ADORATION, detail: the martyred Virgins.

Plate 35

THE ADORATION, detail: the Lamb, surrounded by adoring angels.

Plate 36

THE ADORATION, detail: the Patriarchs, Poets and Philosophers.

Plate 37

THE ADORATION, detail: the great dignitaries of the Church.

Plate 38

THE ADORATION, detail: Confessors and Martyrs.

Plate 39

THE ADORATION, detail: the Apostles.

Plate 40

THE ADORATION, detail: city landscape at top right.

Plate 41

THE ADORATION, detail: city landscape at top center.

Plate 42

THE ADORATION, detail: vegetation and fruit at left background.

Plate 43

THE ADORATION, detail: vegetation and fruit at right background.

Plate 44

THE ADORATION, detail of a Prophet.

Plate 45

THE ADORATION, detail: the Fountain of Life.

Plate 46

JUST JUDGES AND KNIGHTS OF CHRIST. Whole view of both panels. *circa 145 × circa 51*, and *149·2 × 54*. The first panel, the *Just Judges*, was stolen during the night of April 10, 1934; in its place today is a copy by Joseph Van der Veken. In the figures portrayed on both panels some critics have recognized a few of the most distinguished persons of Van Eyck's time: among the *Just Judges*, King Charles IV, the Dukes Jean de Berry and John the Fearless and even the Van Eyck brothers— but this last was surely a flight of fancy. The only indisputable identifications are SS Victor, George and Sebastian who lead the group of the *Knights of Christ*. On this panel one may observe not only Van Eyck's great merits as a painter of animals, but also the advantages he had gained from his journeys to southern countries in capturing the grand sweep and the blue shadows of a magnificent mountain landscape. In this connexion the panel's top right-hand corner is most significant. (See also plates 48, 50 and 51.)

Plate 47

HERMITS AND PILGRIMS. Whole view of both panels. *148·7* × *54·2*. The first group is led by SS Anthony and Paul, while the pilgrims follow a gigantic St Christopher. In the *Hermits* panel, behind some rocks, one perceives St Mary Magdalene and St Mary of Egypt. In the copy of the polyptych in the Antwerp Museum the *Hermits* are seen to follow the *Pilgrims* with whom they form one picture, as is also the case with the *Judges* and the *Knights*. This organization, though admittedly consistant with Münzer's literal description—the oldest of all—does not seem, however, to be the one conceived by Van Eyck. Indeed, there is nothing to prove that the succession of the panels upon the shutters—which are painted on the reverse of the inner-lateral ones— was ever modified: the very attitude of the two *Donors* (plate 67) automatically establishes their position in the open polyptych. The only possible transposition could be the one of the two St Johns, but that would result in the *Pilgrims* changing places with the *Judges*, which is unacceptable. One must conclude therefore that Münzer did not record accurately the order of the various groups, and that the same error was made by the anonymous painter of the great Antwerp canvas. The succession *Hermits—Pilgrims* is therefore the right one and it is the succession that we see in Ghent. An X-ray analysis of the *Pilgrims* panel—and of the other panels with a landscape in the background— showed that the southern flora (date-palms, cypresses, orange-trees, maritime-pines, etc.) is not part of the first coating of paint, but actually covers it. The coating, on the other hand, is perfectly intact and further-more the color-matter with which the southern plants have been painted is exactly the same as the original coating. One must therefore conclude that Van Eyck had painted the shutters before he left for Portugal in 1428, and that he enriched them with exotic plants and flora after his return in 1429. The continuity of the original landscape is clearly visible to the naked eye, as for instance, beyond the trunk of the great isolated palm-tree at right. One should stress, at this point, the boldness of the city landscape in the background (clearly seen in plate 54), and the subtle and disconcertingly modern technique employed by Van Eyck to achieve the effect of light upon the roofs. (See also plates 49 and 52 to 55.)

Plate 48

JUST JUDGES, detail of two figures.

Plate 49

HERMITS, detail of one figure.

Plate 50

KNIGHTS OF CHRIST, detail: St Victor.

Plate 51

KNIGHTS OF CHRIST, detail: heads of two horses.

Plate 52

PILGRIMS, detail of an orange-grove.

Plate 53

HERMITS, detail of center.

Plate 54

PILGRIMS, detail of background beyond the cypress: the city.

Plate 55

PILGRIMS, detail of background: landscape beyond the palm-tree.

THE CLOSED POLYPTYCH
Plate 56

THE ANGEL GABRIEL. This is one of the four panels composing the center zone of the closed polyptych (see plate 7); the other three are visible on plates 57, 60 and 61. The center zone is entirely dedicated to the subject of the Annunciation. Above the lateral compartments, in the upper zone, are two lunettes with the figures of the prophets Zechariah and Micah; in the center of the upper zone, in demi-lunettes, the Erythraean and Cumaean Sibyls. The measurements of the four center-zone panels, from left to right are: *164·8 × 71·7; 212·9 × 37·1; 213·5 × 36·1; 164·8 × 73*. Infra-red rays have revealed, under the present ceiling (painted by Van Eyck), the original compositional drawing of the *Annunciation*, also in Van Eyck's hand. The sketch shows a succession of four trefoliated arches, similar if not identical to those of the lower zone (see plates 66 and 67). This change of scheme could, partially at least, explain the disproportion between the size of the Angel and Virgin (plates 56 and 57) and the height of the room. It is also interesting to note that the basic material for the sketch is not, as in the painting, siccative oil. This proves that Van Eyck was still experimenting with the transition from traditional distemper to siccative oil techniques. The fact that he used both methods must have been known in the fifteenth and sixteenth centuries. Indeed, Marcus van Vaernewijck, writing about the lost predella,

states that it was painted "in watercolors". In this panel the Angel Gabriel, who is holding the symbolic lily, salutes the Virgin with the words, *Ave, gratia plena, D(omi)nus tec(u)m*. The legend is continued from this panel on to the next one (plate 64). True to the logic of the time Mary's reply (plate 57) appears behind her and reads from right to left: *Ecce ancilla D(omi)ni*. (See also plates 57 to 65.)

Plate 57

THE VIRGIN ANNUNCIATE, whole figure. See comment on plate 56.

Plate 58

THE ANGEL GABRIEL, detail of the head.

Plate 59

THE VIRGIN ANNUNCIATE, detail of the hands.

Plate 60

ZECHARIAH AND MICAH. Half-length figures in two lunettes above the lateral compartments of the center zone (see plate 56). The prophets are foretelling the coming of the Redeemer. Their respective scrolls read: "Rejoice greatly, O daughter of Zion; shout, O daughter of Jerusalem: behold, thy King cometh unto thee" (Zechariah, ix, 9); and "Yet out of thee shall he come forth unto me that is to be ruler in Israel" (Micah, v, 2). Between the prophets, in two demi-lunettes, kneel the Erythraean and Cumaean Sibyls, whose scrolls are respectively inscribed with a paraphrase from Vergil's *Aeneid* (vi, 50): "Though thou speaketh not a mortal word thou art inspired by a high divinity" and another from St Augustine's *De Civitate Dei* (xviii, 23): "Thy King will come in the future centuries (to judge) the flesh." The Prophets and the Sybils all belong to a phase of transition, from art as it was before Van Eyck to the master's most typical form of expression. This is already heralded in the bold perspective and fastidious attention to detail. (See also plates 61 to 65.)

Plate 61

CENTRAL PANELS. These two panels, inserted between the *Angel Gabriel* (plate 56) and the *Virgin Annunciate*, link together in the upper zone the four seers and in the center zone the great scene of the Annunciation. See comment on page 18, and following plates 56 and 60. The left panel displays a two-light round-headed window with a view of a Flemish city; the right-hand panel reveals a detail on the wall of Mary's room. (See also plates 62 to 65.)

Plate 62

ERYTHRAEAN SIBYL, detail of the head.

Plate 63

CUMAEAN SIBYL, detail of the head.

Plate 64

CENTRAL PANEL AT LEFT, detail: two-light window with view of Flemish city.

Plate 65

CENTRAL PANEL AT RIGHT, detail: interior of Mary's room, with cupboard, basin and towel.

Plate 66

JOHN THE BAPTIST and JOHN THE EVANGELIST. Whole view of two central panels in the lower zone. *149·1 × 55·1*, and *48·7 × 55·3*. Throughout all his work Van Eyck shows a tendency to imitate sculpture by means of *chiaroscuro* painting as here or, elsewhere, to imitate jewelry and brass. This constant element in his art came from an instinctive feeling for the different material qualities of the objects he was reproducing. In many cases he does not even seem to have required a model, but gives the impression of having directly imagined the matter with which a craftsman could render an image, either in stone or in wood, or in any type of metal. (See also plates 68 and 69.)

Plate 67

THE DONOR AND HIS WIFE, complete view of lateral panels in lower zone. *149·1 × 54·1* and *148·7 × 54·2* The quality of the two superb portraits of Joos Vijdt and Isabelle Borluut is definite proof that—in contrast with the *Prophets* and *Sibyls* —they were painted last, that is, a short time before the polyptych's unveiling. (See also plates 70 to 72.)

Plate 68

JOHN THE BAPTIST, detail of the head.

Plate 69

JOHN THE EVANGELIST, detail of the head.

Plate 70

THE DONOR, detail of the face.

Plate 71

THE DONOR'S WIFE, detail of the face.

Plate 72

THE DONOR, detail of the hands.

Color Plate III

PORTRAIT OF A YOUNG MAN, detail.

Plate 73

CARDINAL ALBERGATI. *Oak, 34·1 × 27·3. Vienna, Kunsthistorisches Museum.* Formerly in the Collection of Archduke Leopold Wilhelm of Austria (1659). Painted in Bruges in 1431–2. Cardinal Niccolò Albergati was sent in 1431 by Pope Martin V on an embassy to Charles VII, King of France, Henry VI, King of England, and Philip the Good, Duke of Burgundy. The picture's four corners were removed about 1720, but repainted before 1783. The Cabinet of Prints at Dresden has a preparatory drawing of this work, executed in silver-point (*21·2 × 18*) in 1431. (See also plate 74.)

Plate 74

CARDINAL ALBERGATI, detail of the head.

Plate 75

PORTRAIT OF A YOUNG MAN (TIMOTHEOS). *Oak, 34·3 × 19. London, National Gallery.* Purchased in 1857 from Karl Ross, a painter, in Munich. On the stone parapet are engraved the words: *Leal Souvenir* (*Leal* standing for *Loyal*). Upon the same block, in paint, are two more inscriptions: *TYM. ΩΘEOC* (Do I fear God?) in Greek characters, and *Actu ano Dni 1432, 10 die octobris a*

ioh de Eyck, in calligraphic characters, signifying that this is a signed work by Van Eyck, dated 1432. The sitter is unknown, though Panofsky identified it as Gilles Binchois, Court-Composer to Philip the Good. The panel is covered with a varnish that has turned yellow with time. (See also plate 76.)

Plate 76

PORTRAIT OF A YOUNG MAN, detail of the head.

Plate 77

MAN IN A TURBAN. *Oak, 25·7 × 19. London, National Gallery.* Formerly in the Collection of the Earl of Arundel, later in the Stafford (*circa* 1720), Broderick (*circa* 1730) and Middleton Collections. Purchased for the National Gallery in 1851. Signed and dated 1433 upon the original frame. The upper border bears the artist's motto: *ALS IXH XAN* ("As I can"). At the foot is Van Eyck's signature: *JOHES DE EYCK ME FECIT ANO MºCCCCº33º 21 OCTOBRIS.* The painting has been thought by some to be Van Eyck's self-portrait, by others a portrait of Van Eyck's father-in-law, but there is no positive evidence to support either theory. With the exception of the face and turban, the panel is covered with a thick coat of varnish. (See also plate 78.)

Plate 78

MAN IN A TURBAN, detail of the head.

Plate 79

THE INCE HALL MADONNA. *Oak, 26·4 × 19·4. Melbourne, Australia, National Gallery of Victoria.* The picture was given as security to someone in Italy in 1619. Later it was said to have been found in Sicily, from where it was acquired for the Duke of Verdura's Collection, perhaps in Rome. From 1854 to 1857 it was certainly in the Weld-Blundell Collection at Ince Hall, hence its name. Signed and dated 1433 on the left background wall: *COMPLETU ANO D MCCCCXXXIIJ P JOHEM DE EYC BRUGIS*, and at right: *ALS IXH XAN*. These inscriptions were in all probability repainted (in 1822 by the restorer G. F. Zink?) on the lines of the original inscriptions upon the frame, which is now lost. The panel's general condition leaves much to be desired. Many parts have been repainted. A copy exists in Spain, at the College of Covarrubias, near Burgos. (See also plate 80.)

Plate 80

THE INCE HALL MADONNA, detail of the window.

Plate 81

THE ANNUNCIATION. *Oak transferred to canvas, 93 × 37. Washington, National Gallery of Art (donated by the Mellon Collection in 1937).* The canvas was discovered in 1819 in a church at Dijon (?); later it went to the Collection of William II, King of Holland; in 1850 it was purchased for the Hermitage Museum in St Petersburg (Leningrad), from which it passed to the Mellon Collection. It is datable about 1434. Gabriel, clad in a red-and-gold brocade cloak, says to Mary: *AVE GRA(TIA) PLENA*; the Virgin, clad in white, replies: *ECCE AN-CILLA D(OMI)NI*. The letters of her reply are inverted. The floor consists of storied panels showing

Samson slaying the Philistines, Samson and Delilah, Samson pulling down the pillars of Dagon's temple, David killing Goliath, etc. The scenes are separated by medallions with the signs of the zodiac: Gemini, Cancer, Leo, Scorpio and Sagittarius. Between the arches in the background, and beneath the *triforium*, are two medallions representing Isaac and Jacob. The glass window shows a full-length figure of Christ, standing on a globe upon which is the word: *ASIA*. Above him are two angels. Frescos on the left and right of the window portray the *Finding of Moses by the daughter of Pharaoh* and *Moses receiving the tables of the law from God*. This panel was the right-hand shutter of an altarpiece, the rest of which has disappeared. (See also plates 82 to 85.)

Plate 82

THE ANNUNCIATION, detail of the Angel Gabriel.

Plate 83

THE ANNUNCIATION, detail of the Virgin.

Plate 84

THE ANNUNCIATION, detail: the upper background wall, with the window and the two frescos of the *Stories of Moses* (see plate 81).

Plate 85

THE ANNUNCIATION, detail: the floor with the *Stories of Samson* (see above, comment on plate 81) and of the stool.

Plate 86

GIOVANNI ARNOLFINI. *Oak, 29 × 20. Berlin, Kaiser Friedrich Museum.* Formerly in the Collection of the Earl of Shrewsbury, sold in

1857, and purchased for the Berlin Museum in 1886 from C. J. Nieuwenhuys of London. Datable about 1434. Giovanni Arnolfini was an Italian merchant originally from Lucca and resident in Bruges from 1421. He was buried there in 1472. Philip the Good bestowed a heraldic title upon him. (See also plate 87.)

Plate 87

THE MARRIAGE OF GIOVANNI ARNOLFINI AND GIOVANNA CENAMI. *Oak, 81·8 × 59·7. London, National Gallery.* Property of Giovanni Arnolfini and of his wife; acquired after 1490 by Don Diego de Guevara, and later presented by him to Archduchess Margaret of Austria, Governess of the Netherlands, at whose death the painting went to Queen Mary of Hungary, also a Governess of the Netherlands. Subsequently the property of the Spanish Royal Family and reported to be in the Alcazar in 1700, 1754 and 1789. In 1815 it was owned by the British General Hay in Brussels, and purchased from him for the National Gallery in 1842. Signed and dated 1434 upon the background wall, above the mirror: *Johannes de Eyck fuit hic 1434.* Giovanni Arnolfini's wife was Giovanna Cenami, the daughter of another merchant from Lucca living in Paris from 1403. She was still alive in 1489. One should note the beautiful round mirror on the far wall, decorated with scenes from the Passion (plate 91). By means of this device we are informed that Arnolfini and his wife are not the only occupants of the room. Two others are either entering or leaving it. Other details represent symbols of married life, such as St Margaret and the lighted candle. (See also plates 88 to 95 and color plate I.)

Plate 88

THE MARRIAGE OF GIOVANNI ARNOLFINI, detail: head of Giovanni Arnolfini.

Color Plate IV

MAN IN A TURBAN

Plate 89

THE MARRIAGE OF GIOVANNI ARNOLFINI, detail: head of Giovanna Cenami.

Plate 90

THE MARRIAGE OF GIOVANNI ARNOLFINI, detail: the hands.

Plate 91

THE MARRIAGE OF GIOVANNI ARNOLFINI, detail: the mirror and Van Eyck's signature.

Plate 92

THE MARRIAGE OF GIOVANNI ARNOLFINI, detail: the chandelier.

Plate 93

THE MARRIAGE OF GIOVANNI ARNOLFINI, detail: the dog.

Plate 94

THE MARRIAGE OF GIOVANNI ARNOLFINI, detail: the window and apples.

Plate 95

THE MARRIAGE OF GIOVANNI ARNOLFINI, detail: the pattens.

Plates 96–97

THE MADONNA TRIPTYCH (also known as VIRGIN WITH CHILD, SS CATHERINE AND MICHAEL AND DONOR). *Oak. Inner measurements: 27·5 × 21·5; outer: 27·5 × 37·5. Dresden, Gemäldegalerie.* An escutcheon in the frame justifies the belief that the triptych was commissioned by a member of the noble family Giustiniani of Genoa. Formerly in the Collection of Everard Jabach, in Paris (N.266 in the inventory drawn up on July 17, 1696?). Purchased in 1765 for the Dresden Museum. Datable about 1435. In the central panel the Virgin and Child; the left panel portrays St Michael protecting the kneeling donor and the right one, St Catherine. The Child holds a long white scroll bearing a text from St Matthew (ix, 29). Many of the piers in the background have storied capitals. The throne's principals are crowned by bronze figures representing Abraham, Isaac, David and Goliath, a pelican and a phoenix. The frame of the inner panels bears Latin inscriptions in Van Eyck's hand. The outer faces of the shutters show an Annunciation in *chiaroscuro* (plate 100), in which the archangel and the Virgin are represented as statues of stone standing on pedestals inside two rectangular niches. (See also plates 98 to 100.)

Plate 98

THE MADONNA TRIPTYCH. Interior of the two shutter panels, with St Michael protecting the Donor and St Catherine.

Plate 99

THE MADONNA TRIPTYCH, detail: the central panel with the Virgin and Child.

Plate 100

THE MADONNA TRIPTYCH, detail: the outer shutters, with the Annunciation.

Plate 101

PORTRAIT OF A GOLDSMITH. *Oak, 174·4 × 155·5. Rumania, Baron Bruckenthal Collection.* Datable about 1435. With the exception of the face and hands the panel's condition is unsatisfactory. The blue of the man's head-gear, for instance, has undergone many harmful chemical alterations. This portrait and that of Jan De Leeuw (plate 120), Dean of the Brussels goldsmiths, proves that Van Eyck was acquainted with the members of that corporation in Brussels and also, undoubtedly, in Bruges.

Plate 102

THE LUCCA MADONNA. *Oak, 65·5 × 49·5. Frankfurt, Staedel Institute.* Formerly in the Collections of Charles-Louis of Bourbon, Duke of Lucca; of the dealer Nieuenhuys at Brussels (1841–2); of William II, King of Holland, from whom it was purchased for the Frankfurt Museum in 1850. Datable 1435 and exceptionally well preserved. To be considered one of Van Eyck's purest masterpieces.

Plate 103

THE LUCCA MADONNA, detail of the Virgin and Child.

Plate 104

THE ANNUNCIATION. *Oak, 39 × 24* (each panel). Lugano, Collection of Baron Von Thyssen (Villa Favorita). Formerly in the collection of a noble French family. Datable about 1435. The frames of these two outer shutters of a lost triptych bear the following inscriptions: Above the angel: AVE GRA(TIA) PLENA D(OMI)N(U)S TECU(M) B(E)N(E)D(I)C(T)A TU I(N) MULIE(RIBUS); above the Virgin: ECCE ANCILLA DOMINI FIAT MIHI S(E)C(UN)D(U)M V(ER)BU(M) TU(UM). The figures of the two holy characters, though very similar to those of the *Madonna Triptych*, are perhaps the only *trompe-l'oeil* of the fifteenth century. This plate shows the left-hand shutter with the Angel Gabriel. (See also plate 105.)

Plate 105

THE ANNUNCIATION. Right-hand shutter with the Virgin. See comment on plate 104.

Plate 106

VIRGIN AND CHILD WITH CHANCELLOR ROLIN. *Oak, 66 × 62. Paris, Louvre.* Commissioned by Chancellor Nicholas Rolin, founder of the Hotel-Dieu in Beaune. The portrait was donated to Autun Cathedral either by the Chancellor or by his son Jean Rolin (Bishop of Autun from 1436). There it remained until 1800, and that is why it is also known as *The Autun Virgin*. In 1800 A. Lenoir transferred it to the Louvre. Datable about 1436. Many towns have been suggested in an attempt to identify the city in the background: Lyons, Autun, Liege, Maastricht, Utrecht, Prague and others, but the mystery has not yet been solved. The three storied capitals above the Chancellor's head represent the *Expulsion of Adam and Eve from the Garden of Eden, The sacrifice of Cain and Abel* and *Noah's drunkenness*. Along the edge of the Virgin's mantle runs the inscription: *Exaltata sum in Libano*. Nicholas Rolin, born in Autun in 1376, was appointed Chancellor of the Burgundy States by Philip the Good on December 3, 1422; he died in Antwerp on January 18, 1462. This painting has had an enormous influence on art, as is proved, for example, by Roger Van der Weyden's *Virgin and St Luke*, now in Boston. (See also plates 107 to 110.)

Plate 107

VIRGIN AND CHILD WITH CHANCELLOR ROLIN, detail of the Virgin and Child.

Plate 108

VIRGIN AND CHILD WITH CHANCELLOR ROLIN, detail of the Chancellor's head.

Plate 109

VIRGIN AND CHILD WITH CHANCELLOR ROLIN, detail of the background with town and landscape.

Plate 110

VIRGIN AND CHILD WITH CHANCELLOR ROLIN, detail of the central view, between the two columns.

Plate 111

VIRGIN WITH CANON VAN DER PAELE. *Oak, 122 × 157. Bruges, Museum voor Schone Kunsten.* Painted for the Church of St Donatian in Bruges, at the donor's request. In 1567 Guicciardini wrote that it was the property of the church. Signed and dated 1436 upon the original frame: *Hoc op(us) fecit fieri mag(iste)r georgi(u)s de pala hui(u)s ecclesi(a)e canoni(cu)s p(er) johanne(m) de eyck pictore(m): et fundavit hic duas capell(an)ias de gremio chori domini M⁰CCCC⁰xxx iiij; c(om)p(le)t(um) ann(no) 1436.* The frame bears two escutcheons, one of the Canon's family and the second perhaps of the Carlijns family to which his mother belonged. The Virgin's throne is decorated with figures of *Adam and Eve, The Death of Abel* and *Samson slaying the lion.* A copy by Gerard Horenbout (?), formerly in the church of Watervliet-lez-Eeklo (Eastern Flanders), is in Antwerp. (See also comment on page 31 and plates 112 to 119.)

Plate 112

VIRGIN WITH CANON VAN DER PAELE, detail: *The Death of Abel*, one of the sculptured groups decorating the Virgin's throne.

Plate 113

VIRGIN WITH CANON VAN DER PAELE, detail of the Child.

Plate 114

VIRGIN WITH CANON VAN DER PAELE, detail: face of St Donatian.

Plate 115

VIRGIN WITH CANON VAN DER PAELE, detail: face of the donor.

Plate 116

VIRGIN WITH CANON VAN DER PAELE, detail: head of St Donatian.

Plate 117

VIRGIN WITH CANON VAN DER PAELE, detail: armor of St George.

Plate 118

VIRGIN WITH CANON VAN DER PAELE, detail of the storied capitals.

Plate 119

VIRGIN WITH CANON VAN DER PAELE, detail of the Virgin's mantle and the carpet.

Plate 120

JAN DE LEEUW. *Oak, 33 × 26. Vienna, Kunsthistorisches Museum* (from 1783). An inscription in Dutch on the original frame incorporates the sitter's name, the artist's signature and the date of execution, 1436. The text is probably apocryphal but the information it contains

seems plausible. Jan de Leeuw, a goldsmith, was born in Bruges on October 12, 1401, and became Dean of his Guild in Brussels in 1441. Nothing, therefore, appears to confute the sitter's identification and the date of 1436.

Plate 121

BALDOVINO DE LANNOY. *Oak, 26 × 20. Berlin, Kaiser Friedrich Museum* (from 1902). Formerly in the Collection of the Marquess of Coccapane in Modena. Datable 1437. The sitter's identity has been established due to a drawing in the town library of Arras. Baldovino, or Baldwin, of Lannoy was born in 1386–7 and was appointed Governor of Lille in 1423 and Captain of the Castle of Mortagne in 1428. That same year he was sent to Portugal with Philip the Good's official delegation to beg the hand of Princess Isabella. When the lady entered Bruges on January 10, 1430, the Duke of Burgundy founded the Order of the Golden Fleece, which then was awarded only to the members of Philip's family and to three gentlemen who had directly contributed to bring about the marriage. They were: André de Thoulongeon, ex-Ambassador of John the Fearless in Lisbon; Jean de Roubaix, head of the mission to Portugal, and Baldwin de Lannoy, who is here portrayed wearing the enameled gold collar of the Order.

Plate 122

ST BARBARA. *Antwerp, Museum voor Schone Kunsten. 34·2 × 18·6.* From three inscriptions—one in long-hand and two printed—on the back of the picture we learn that this work was part of the Joz. Enschedé Collection at Harlem in 1769, then the property of J. Cornelis Ploos at Amstel, Oyen, and eventually purchased by M. F. van Ertborn who bequeathed it to the Antwerp Museum in 1841. Carel Van Mander recorded that Lucas de Heere owned "a small female portrait" against a "small landscape", and that it was "an unfinished work". These data are too vague to confirm their identification as Van Eyck's drawing, which is signed and dated at the foot of the original frame: *JOHES DE EYCK ME FECIT, 1437.* Rather than a drawing it should be described as an unfinished painting: the oak panel is covered with a preparatory coating of chalk and animal glue, and inserted in a frame that was definitely intended for a Van Eyck painting. The master imitated marble, and the letters of the signature and date give the impression of having been carved in that stone. Presumably unforeseen circumstances, such as the donor's death, prevented Van Eyck from finishing this work. The few gray-blue brushstrokes in the sky are clearly painted later than the fifteenth century. *St Barbara* is the only drawing attributed to Van Eyck with any certainty, and it shows all the characteristics of a painting. (See also plate 123.)

Plate 123

ST BARBARA, detail: men at work on the right side of the Cathedral.

Plate 124

THE VIRGIN AT THE FOUNTAIN. *Oak, 19 × 12·2. Antwerp. Museum voor Schone Kunsten.* Formerly the property of Margaret of Austria, Governess of the Netherlands. Until 1830 in the possession of the Curate of Dikkelvenne, in Eastern Flanders. In that year it was purchased by M. F. van Ertborn, who bequeathed it to the Antwerp Museum in 1841. Signed and dated 1439 upon the original frame: at the head: *ALS IXH XAN*; at the foot: *JOHES DE EYCK ME FECIT C(OM)PLEVIT AN(N)O 1439.* A copy of this painting was owned by William II, King of Holland and was later sold in England. Another copy, slightly altered, is kept in Berlin. (See also plate 125.)

Plate 125

THE VIRGIN AT THE FOUNTAIN, detail of the central group.

Plate 126

MARGHARITA VAN EYCK. *Oak, 32 × 26. Bruges, Museum voor Schone Kunsten.* Formerly in the St Luke Chapel at Bruges and the property of the Guild of Painters and Saddlers. Purchased in 1808 by Pierre Van Lede, who donated it to the Museum. Signed and dated 1439, and inscribed upon the original frame. At the head: *CO(N)IUX M(EU)S IOH(ANN)ES ME C(OM)PLEVIT AN(N)O 1439 17 IUNII*; at the foot: *ETAS MEA TRIGINTA TRIU(M) AN(N)-ORU(M) ALS IXH XAN.* As was his custom, Van Eyck painted these words to look as if they had been carved in stone—here in porphyry. From the inscription one may deduce that his wife Margaret was born in 1406. No other facts are known about her. (See also plate 127.)

Plate 127

MARGHARITA VAN EYCK, detail of the face.

LOST PAINTINGS

RELIGIOUS SUBJECTS

HELL, in the predella of the *Adoration of the Lamb* altarpiece at Ghent, as described by Marcus van Vaernewijck (1568) and Carel van Mander (1617).

JUST JUDGES, part of the right-hand shutter of the Ghent altarpiece, stolen in 1934.

ADORATION OF THE MAGI (?) and ANNUNCIATION, central panel and reverse of the two New York shutters with the *Crucifixion* and the *Last Judgement*. (See Attributed Paintings and plate 136.)

THE WASHINGTON ANNUNCIATION (plate 81), central and left-hand panel.

THE LUGANO ANNUNCIATION (plates 104–5): perhaps the central panel. However, the painting might have been conceived from the beginning as a simple diptych.

HEAD OF CHRIST AS KING OF KINGS. The original seems that mentioned in the 1652 inventory of the Forchoudt concern at Antwerp. Also known because of copies in the Berlin (see plate 148) and Munich museums.

HEAD OF CHRIST AS THE SAVIOR, sold on October 16, 1671, by the Forchoudt Company of Antwerp to Lantsinger.

THE ANNUNCIATION, recorded by B. Facio (1456) in the Collection of Alphonse V, King of Naples. The outer shutters portray SS John the Baptist and Jerome; on the reverse are portraits of Battista Lomellino and his wife.

THE ANNUNCIATION, mentioned in an inventory (1675?) of the Forchoudt Company of Antwerp. *86·5 × 65*. Because of the considerable difference in dimensions it is unlikely that this panel was one and the same as the lost Washington *Annunciation* (plate 81).

SMALL VIRGIN, recorded in 1649 in the inventory of the worldly goods of Abraham Matthys of Antwerp. Perhaps the same as the *Madonna in a Church* in Berlin? (plate 1).

ST JEROME, recorded in 1492 in the inventory of Lorenzo the Magnificent.

ST GEORGE AND THE DRAGON, purchased in 1445 by Alphonse V, King of Naples.

NON-RELIGIOUS SUBJECTS

WOMAN COMING OUT OF A STEAMY BATH, mentioned by Facio (1456) in the Collection of Cardinal Ottaviano. A copy of this was painted by Willem van Haecht for a *Cabinet de Peinture* (small picture gallery) (1628) belonging to the Antwerp collector, Cornelis Van der Geest, who died in 1638. The copy was formerly in the Lord Huntingfield Collection at Heveningham and is now part of the Van Berg Collection in New York.

A HUNT ORGANIZED BY PHILIP THE GOOD. Copies in France at the Versailles Museum and at the Chateau of Azay-le-Rideau.

LANDSCAPE WITH AN OTTER HUNT, recorded by Marcantonio Michiel (before 1550) in the collection of the Padua philosopher Leonico Tomeo.

LANDOWNER REVIEWING HIS ACCOUNTS WITH HIS AGENT. Recorded by M. Michiel (before 1550) in the possession of Niccolò Lampugnano of Milan. The work, portraying two men at half-length, is believed to have been painted in 1440.

THE WORLD, described by Facio as: *mundi comprehensio, orbiculari forma*, painted by Van Eyck for Philip the Good (1456).

A MARSERINGE (?) and a MARCHERINGE (?), recorded in the Antwerp Collections of Dierick Ketgen (1660) and Johannes van Hove (1676).

PORTRAITS

ISABELLA OF PORTUGAL, painted during Van Eyck's mission to Lisbon in 1428–9.

PORTUGUESE LADY, formerly in the Collection of Don Diego de Guevara (after 1490) and of Margaret of Austria, Governess of the Netherlands. Possibly a second portrait of Isabella of Portugal, third wife of Philip the Good.

SMALL PORTRAIT OF LADY IN A LANDSCAPE, recorded by Carel van Mander in the Collection of Lucas de Heere at the end of the sixteenth century. Perhaps the abovementioned St Barbara. (See plate 122.)

PORTRAIT OF MAN AND PORTRAIT OF WOMAN, mentioned in the inventory of Pierre-Paul Rubens' Collection at Antwerp in 1640.

PORTRAIT, sold on May 13, 1654, by the Forchoudt Company at Antwerp.

Three other paintings are mentioned as the work of Hubrecht van Eyck. These references, of course, all date after 1565 when Lucas de Heere's Ode was published.

VIRGIN AND CHILD, AN ANGEL AND ST BERNARD, recorded in 1595 in the Collection of Archduke Ernest of Austria, as a work by Rupert Van Eyck.

NATIVITY, sold by the Forchoudt Company at Antwerp in May, 1660.

VIRGIN AND CHILD, in the Jabach Collection at Cologne in 1696.

PAINTINGS ATTRIBUTED TO
JAN VAN EYCK

Plates 128–130

THE THREE MARYS AT THE
SEPULCHER. *Vierhouten (Holland)*.
Collection of D. G. van Beuningen.
Panel, 71·5 × 89, attributed to
Hubrecht van Eyck as a work
executed before 1420, by W. H. J.
Weale, Hulin de Loo, Beenken and
Baldass. Attributed to Jan Van Eyck
by Renders and Lavallaye.

Plates 131–135

TURIN BOOK OF HOURS. This is the
part preserved today in Turin's
Museo Civico, and formerly known
as *Heures de Milan* (from the beginning of the nineteenth century until
1933 it was part of the Trivulzio Collection in Milan). It was a book of
miniatures designed or painted for
the Duc de Berry between 1380 and
1390. The making of the book took
some fifty years. The miniatures
were done by several artists and one
outstanding group among them has
been attributed alternatively to
Hubrecht and Jan Van Eyck. Jan
is believed to have been responsible
for the following miniatures: *God the
Father among the Angles* and a *Pietà*,
both part of a section of the Book
formerly in the Turin National Library and destroyed by fire in 1904;
Christ on the Mount of Olives and a
Crucifixion, formerly in the Trivulzio
Collection, Milan and now in Turin.
This attribution, suggested by P.
Durrieu Hulin de Loo, Friedländer
and Renders, is contested by Hooge-
werf and Lyna. Durrieu and Hulin

de Loo attribute to Hubrecht the
following miniatures: *The kiss of
Judas, SS Julian and Martha in a
storm, Mary among the Virgins, Duke
William of Bavaria on the beach at
Walcheren* (all these works were
destroyed in the 1904 fire at Turin),
the *Discovery of the Cross* (plate 131),
the *Requiem Mass* (plate 132) and *The
Birth of St John* (plates 133–5, showing the initial letters of these two
pages). The last two works were
part of the Trivulzio Collection and
are now in Turin's Museo Civico.
The dimensions of each page are
28 × 19.

Plates 136–140

CRUCIFIXION and THE LAST
JUDGEMENT. *Oak transferred to
canvas. Dimensions of each painting 56·5 ×
19·7. New York, Metropolitan Museum
of Art.* The two shutters were
purchased from a Spanish convent
by Prince Tatischev, an Ambassador
of Tsar Nicholas I of Russia; after
1845 they were moved to the
Hermitage Museum in Leningrad
and sold to the Metropolitan
Museum in 1933. The central
panel, which was lost, was said
to portray an *Adoration of the Magi*.
Perhaps a copy of this work is
drawing No. 4244 in the Berlin
Museum. The work is datable about
1424. The two panels have been
attributed to Jan Van Eyck (C. Justi,
1887; Friedländer, 1924–37), to
Hubrecht (Beenken, 1941; H. B.
Wehle and M. Salinger, 1947), to both

brothers (Passavant, 1841), to Peter Christus (Waagen, 1845; Crowe and Cavalcaselle 1872) and to the "Master of the Turin Book of Hours" (Dvorak, 1918; L. Baldass 1951). Because of the many attributions in this volume the two paintings come under the heading "Attributed Paintings", although I am convinced that these are autograph works by Jan Van Eyck. The majority of old paintings sold by the Soviet Union to the United States of America are oils transferred from wood on to canvas, and the same is true of these works. In this case it is deplorable since the process has irreparably destroyed every trace of painting on the back of the shutters. Passavant recorded that in 1841 one could still make out two figures standing on pedestals: presumably those of the Virgin and Gabriel, similar to the Dresden and Lugano *Annunciations* (plates 100, 104–5). On the frame of the *Crucifixion* is a text from Isaiah (liii, 6–12). In the *Last Judgement*, Christ, addressing the Chosen, says: *Venite Benedicti p(at)ris mei*. The Archangel Michael, tells the damned: *Ite vos maledicti in ignem eternum*. Inscribed on the wings of Death are the words: *Chaos magnu(m)* and *Umbra mortis*. The frame bears some Biblical quotations (Apocalypse, xx, 13, xxi, 3–4; Deuteronomy, xxxii, 23–4). In the Berlin Museum there is a copy of the *Last Judgement* by Petrus Christus, signed and dated 1452.

Plates 141–142

CRUCIFIXION. *Berlin, Kaiser Friedrich Museum. Panel, 43 × 26.* Attributed to Jan Van Eyck by Tschudi and Friedländer and by the author; believed by Beenken to be a work by Hubrecht.

Plate 143

MADONNA WITH TWO SAINTS AND CARTHUSIAN MONK. *Paris, Rothschild Collection. Panel transferred to canvas, 47 × 61.* Attributed to Jan Van Eyck by Friedländer, Tolnay, Beenken and Baldass.

Plates 144–145

ANNUNCIATION. *New York, Metropolitan Museum of Art. Panel, 77·5 × 66·4.* Attributed to Hubrecht Van Eyck by Panofsky and Baldass, at least in so far as the composition is concerned.

Plate 146

ST JEROME STUDYING. *Detroit, Institute of Arts. Panel, 20 × 13.* Attributed to Jan Van Eyck by Valentiner and Baldass.

Plate 147

VIRGIN WITH ABBOT NICHOLAS VAN MAELBEKE, PROVOST OF ST MARTIN'S. *Paris, Private Collection. Panel, 172 × 99.* Also called *The Ypres Madonna*, and attributed to Jan Van Eyck by Weale, Friedländer, Winkler and Baldass.

Plate 148

HEAD OF CHRIST. *British Private Collection* (O. S. Swinburne Fund); exhibited at The Hague in 1923 and at Newcastle-upon-Tyne in 1951. *Panel, 24 × 16.* Attributed to Jan Van Eyck by Conway. Friedländer and Baldass.

Plate 149

HEAD OF CHRIST (as KING OF KINGS). *Berlin, Kaiser Friedrich Museum. Panel, 44 × 32.* Like the one in Munich, this is probably also a copy of Jan Van Eyck's painting mentioned in the Forchoudt inventory of 1652, and to which I have referred in Lost Paintings.

Plate 150

ECCLESIASTIC. *Montauban, Ingres Museum. Panel, 26 × 19.* Attributed to Jan Van Eyck by Friedländer and Beenken, to Hubrecht Van Eyck by Durand-Greville.

Plate 151

PORTRAIT OF A MAN. *Philadelphia, Pennsylvania Museum of Art. Panel, 18·4 × 14·3.* Attributed to Jan Van Eyck by Weale, Valentiner and Lord Conway.

Plate 152

FRAGMENT OF PORTRAIT OF A DONOR. *Leipzig, Museum der Bildende Künste. Panel, 26·4 × 19·5.* Attributed to Hubrecht Van Eyck by Friedländer and Beenken.

Plates 153–155

PORTRAIT OF A MAN HOLDING PINK. *Berlin, Kaiser Friedrich Museum. Panel, 40 × 31.* Attributed to Jan Van Eyck by Friedländer; to Hubrecht by Weale, Brockwell, Kaemmerer, Seek and Schenk.

Plates 156–160

STIGMATIZATION OF ST FRANCIS. *Turin, Galleria Sabauda. Panel, 29·5 × 33·5.* Attributed alternatively to Jan Van Eyck, to his school, or even considered a copy of the Philadelphia painting shown in plate 4. Friedländer attributes it to Jan Van Eyck and dates it approximately 1480. This attribution has recently been supported by C. Aru and E. de Gerardon, and also by Ragghianti who considers the work an original copy of the Philadelphia masterpiece.

THE MADMAN. *Vienna, Kunsthistorisches Museum. Panel, 36 × 24.* Attributed to Jan Van Eyck by Brockwell.

JOHN THE FEARLESS. *Antwerp, Museum voor Schone Kunsten. Panel, 21 × 14.* Attributed to Hubrecht Van Eyck by Beenken.

LOCATION OF PAINTINGS

ANTWERP

MUSEUM VOOR SCHONE KUN-
STEN

St Barbara (plates 122, 123).
The Virgin at the Fountain (plates 124, 125).

BERLIN

KAISER FRIEDRICH MUSEUM

Madonna in a church (plates 1, 2, 3).
Giovanni Arnolfini (plate 86).
Baldovino de Lannoy (plate 121).
Crucifixion (plates 141, 142; attribution).
Head of Christ as King of Kings (plate 149; attribution).
Portrait of man holding pink (plates 153, 154, 155; attribution).

BRUGES

MUSEUM VOOR SCHONE KUN-
STEN

Virgin with Canon van der Paele (plates 111, 112, 113, 114, 115, 116, 117, 118, 119).
Margharita Van Eyck (plates 126, 127).

DETROIT

INSTITUTE OF ARTS

St Jerome Studying (plate 146; attribution).

DRESDEN

GEMÄLDEGALERIE

The Madonna Triptych (plates 96-7, 98, 99, 100).

FRANKFURT

STEÄDELSCHES KUNSTINSTI-
TUT

The Lucca Madonna (plates 102, 103).

GHENT

CATHEDRAL OF ST BAVON

The Adoration of the Sacred Lamb (color plate I–II and plates 7–72). General view of the exterior, plate 7; general view of the interior, plates 8–9; *God*, plates 10, 11, 12, 13, 18; *The Virgin*, plates 14, 16; *John the Baptist*, plates 15, 17, 19; *Angels playing and singing*, plates 20, 21, 22, 23, 24, 25; *Two Biblical Episodes*, plate 26; *Adam and Eve*, plates 27, 28, 29, 30, 31; *The Adoration*, plates 32–3, 34, 35, 36, 37, 38, 39, 40, 41, 42, 43, 44, 45; *Just Judges* and *Knights of Christ*, plates 46, 48, 50, 51; *Hermits and Pilgrims*, plates 47, 49, 52, 53, 54, 55; *The Angel Gabriel*, plates 56, 58; *The Virgin*, plates 57, 59; *Zechariah and Micah*, plate 60; Central panels, exterior: plates 61, 64, 65; *The Erythraean Sibyl*, plate 62; *The Cumaean Sibyl*, plate 63; *John the Baptist and John the Evangelist*, plates 66, 68, 69; *The Donor and his Wife*, plates 67, 70, 71, 72.

LEIPZIG

MUSEUM DER BILDENDE
KÜNSTE

Fragment of Portrait of a Donor (plate 152; attribution).

LONDON

NATIONAL GALLERY
Portrait of a young man (color plate III and plates 75, 76).
Man in a turban (Color plate IV and plates 77, 78).
The Marriage of Giovanni Arnolfini and Giovanna Cenami (plates 87, 88, 89, 90, 91, 92, 93, 94, 95).

LUGANO

VON THYSSEN COLLECTION
Annunciation (plates 104, 105).

MELBOURNE

NATIONAL GALLERY OF VICTORIA
The Ince Hall Madonna (plates 79, 80).

MONTAUBAN (FRANCE)

INGRES MUSEUM
Ecclesiastic (plate 150; attribution).

NEW YORK

METROPOLITAN MUSEUM OF ART
Crucifixion and *The Last Judgement* (plates 136, 137, 138, 139, 140; attribution).
Annunciation (plates 144, 145; attribution).

PARIS

LOUVRE
Virgin with Chancellor Rolin (plates 106, 107, 108, 109, 110).

PHILADELPHIA

PENNSYLVANIA MUSEUM OF ART
The Stigmatization of St Francis (plates 4, 5, 6).
Portrait of a man (plate 151; attribution).

PRIVATE COLLECTION

Virgin with Abbot Van Maelbeke (plate 147; attribution).

ROTHSCHILD COLLECTION
Madonna with two saints and Carthusian Monk (plate 143; attribution).

RUMANIA

BARON BRUCKENTHAL COLLECTION
Portrait of a Goldsmith (plate 101).

TURIN

MUSEO CIVICO
Book of Hours; Discovery of the Cross (plate 131; attribution).
Requiem Mass (plates 132, 134; attribution).
The Birth of St John (plates 133, 135; attribution).

GALLERIA SABAUDA
The Stigmatization of St Francis (plates 156, 157, 158, 159, 160; attribution).

UNITED KINGDOM

PRIVATE COLLECTION
Head of Christ (plate 148; attribution).

VIENNA

KUNSTHISTORISCHES MUSEUM
Cardinal Albergati (plates 73, 74).
Jan de Leeuw (plate 120).

VIERHOUTEN (HOLLAND)

VAN BEUNINGEN COLLECTION
The Three Marys at the Sepulcher (plates 128, 129, 130; attribution).

WASHINGTON

NATIONAL GALLERY OF ART
Annunciation (plates 81, 82, 83, 84, 85).

SELECTED CRITICISM

That famous Jan of Bruges, who honored the art of painting.

> CIRIACO DE' PIZZICOLLI OF ANCONA
> *Commentari delle antiche cose*, circa 1450.

The king of painters, whose perfect and accurate works shall never be forgotten . . .

> JEAN LEMAIRE DE BELGES
> *La Couronne Margaritique*, 1504–11.

Jan of Bruges who opened the eyes of those painters; but they, by imitating only his manner and not thinking any further, have left our churches full of works which do not resemble good and natural things, but are only dressed in beautiful colors.

> L. LOMBARD
> In a letter to Vasari, April 27, 1563.

Jan Van Eyck, a prince among all painters, also left a memory of his art in Bruges.

> M. VAN VAERNEWIJCK
> *Den Spiegel der Nederlander Audheyt*, 1568.

The paintings in question are simply some kind of shutters, very narrow and six in number . . . this sort of ancient shutter of a very unsightly shape. . . . They (the French in 1794) paid so little attention to the shutters that they left them in the church, as objects of little value. One did not know what to do with these odd pieces, which seemed to claim no other merit than their age and the name of he who had painted them.

> J. LE SURRE
> Vicar-General of Ghent, in a letter to the Governor of Eastern Flanders,
> July 7, 1817.

The spirit can dwell upon it eternally, without reaching the full depth of that which it evokes. The eye may enjoy it as well, without exhausting the extraordinary wealth of pleasure that it bestows, or of the lessons that it teaches us.

E. FROMENTIN
Les Maitres d'autrefois, 1876.

The naturalism of the Van Eycks, which art historians are known to consider as an element preluding the Renaissance, should be seen rather as an accomplished development of the spirit of the late Middle Ages. It contains the same naturalistic representation of the divine that we have observed in everything related to the cult of saints, in the sermons of John Brugman, in the elaborate contemplations of Gerson, in the description of the infernal punishment undergone by Dionysius the Carthusian. . . . The art of the Van Eycks, as far as its contents are concerned, is still entirely medieval. It brings with it no new ideas: it is a terminal, a final point. The conceptual system of the Middle Ages was a complete construction which rose up to the sky; the only things one could add to it were color and ornaments. . . . (About the *Virgin with Chancellor Rolin*): The meticulous accuracy brought into the treatment of cloths, of the marble constituting the flagstones and columns, the gleam of the window-panes, the Chancellor's missal, would appear pedantic in any other painter than Van Eyck. . . . But only outside the open hall enclosing the principal figures, does the love for details reach an extreme point. . . . And now the miracle takes place: in all this, contrary to what was stated by Michelangelo's pupil, unity and harmony are never lost.

J. HUIZINGA
Autumn of the Middle Ages, 1928.

His gaze is so penetrating that he can rebuild the human body and make it visible under its clothes, something that had never bothered the miniaturists before him. With the same power he conquers all that is real in a landscape, in light, in the cohesion of objects, of flora, of rocks, of cloths and of metals, just as he captures the reality of individual man and the solidity of his constitution. . . . He knows cloth as well as a weaver, architecture as a master mason, earth as a geographer, flora as a botanist. . . . With the passing of years, Van Eyck's art evolves towards a clearer sobriety. His compositions acquire a greater simplicity, placidity, plasticity, economy of means, dignity. . . . Jan Van Eyck was faithful to the Church, and his even nature was not tormented by the dichotomy between sensual pleasure and his function of translating this world of the senses for the benefit of the faithful.

M. J. FRIEDLÄNDER
Ancient Painting in the Netherlands, 1937.

Van Eyck's genius is still closely bound to the Middle Ages and to his own century, that is obvious; but it is also especially true of all that concerns his poetic feeling and perhaps even a certain philosophy of the microcosm. . . . Gradually, as the principles of monumental art slowly dissolve, and painting replaces sculpture as a means of knowledge of the universe, the taste for what is infinitely small develops more and more. But could one ever confuse this passion for a fastidiously executed detail with that attitude of supine passivity commonly described as realism? If we were to see reality with those eyes, our senses would reel. In contemplating those immense and tiny townscapes in the public squares of which human beings come and go who are barely perceptible, and yet built to perform with thoroughness all that life demands of them, we may well ask whether the artist's thought did not coincide, here, with that of the astrologers, of the mystics, and whether he did not wish to insert, in God's world, a painted world which would reproduce its figures in infinitesimal measurements, just as the human figure, placed in the center of the Zodiacal circle, represents the microcosm of universal being. I believe that evidence of this can be found in the circular, concave mirror hanging from the wall of the nuptial chamber in which Arnolfini and his wife exchange their oath of loyalty. . . . In a sense, every reality is mysterious for Van Eyck; he confronts his objects as if he had just discovered them for the first time: he studies them as if he intended, with poetic patience, to capture from them the solution to some riddle, as if he meant to cast a spell upon them and infuse in their images a second, silent life. Everything is for him unique and, in the true sense of the word, singular. In such a universe, in which nothing is interchangeable, the accessory and the inanimate acquire the same physiognomical value as a face.

H. FOCILLON
Art of the West, 1938.

Jan Van Eyck, the Flemish master, discovers (or uncovers?) the eternity of things in a universe as unchangeable, as terse and as hard as crystal.

His greatness is to be found in the conscious limits which he imposes to himself, and in his tenacious search for a new, lapidary and expressive form of the universe.

In his art there is no development as such. He repeats himself and, by so doing, he confirms his ideal.

In spite of this clarity of plastic form and of the realistic, almost sensuous effect produced by the brightness of the matter, the general view (of the *Virgin with Canon van der Paele*) resplendent with deep reds, with velvety blues, with yellow-golds and olive-greens, all distributed in great splashes upon the figures' clothes and again, in lesser proportions, on the carpet's adornments—is close to an elusive dream.

Thus Van Eyck's pictures taught the men of the late Middle Ages that joy of living is no sin, for not only is it licit but it emanates from God. The hierarchy which, in the Middle Ages, subordinated the earthly world to the heavenly one is abolished. An empiric world, the smallest particle of which radiates divine substance, has replaced the cosmos, where everything had its pre-established place.

Even in his portraits, Jan Van Eyck was not content to portray simply an ephemeral personality. He consciously transported man into a state of beatitude, out of time, free from daily vicissitudes. There is a certain contradiction between Van Eyck's

66

tendency to spiritualize in general his figures and the fastidious realism with which he observed their physical appearance.

CHARLES DE TONAY
The "Master of Flémalle" and the Van Eyck brothers, 1939.

A painting by Van Eyck is as perfect in itself as a cut crystal resplendent with deep colors. No movement, no suffering, but rather the happy unfolding of an existence. By this quality he ennobled all that he touched. A fruit upon a window-sill becomes like a jewel, a bronze platter or a chandelier are transformed into precious objects. Especially in his interior, nothing looks common.

H. BEENKEN
Hubrecht and Jan van Eyck, 1941.

It is senseless to speak of realism or idealism in connexion with artists who gave a form to the reality which they lived (the late Middle Ages). Van Eyck and his successors were no more realists than they were idealists, exactly like Sluter, Dufay and Ockeghem, who built the cathedrals of Ghent and Antwerp, and the poets of *Elckerlyk* and *Mariken van Nieuweghem*. They were objectivists in the fullest sense of the world: they recorded, as good craftsmen, all that they saw exactly as they saw it, and this they did with an apparent objectivity that we shall never find elsewhere in such fullness of measure, neither before nor after them. . . . But everything they saw was permeated with the supernatural. This is what defines the often neglected difference between reality as represented by the Flemish primitives and the more strictly *bourgeois* reality which inspired the Dutch masters of the seventeenth century. From here, too, stems the total contradiction between the so-called realism of Van Eyck, Van der Weyden and Van der Goes on the one side, and on the other that physical approach, foreign to all spirituality, towards which the naturalists of the nineteenth century gravitated, whilst noisily expounding their philosophical theories.

A. STUBBE
Van Eyck and the Gothic, 1947.

Van Eyck's art represents the highest peak achieved by the ancient masters of the Netherlands. This is proven by the artistic individuality of a master who did so much to improve easel-painting, and by the so very expressive power of his pictures. No one has ever succeeded in ensuring the intensity and harmony of his brilliant, deep colors. The great central panel of his Ghent polyptych shows most clearly the craftsmanship of his hand. . . . In spite of everything the meaning of Jan's art can be correctly appreciated only if one remembers that his technique was adopted by the French and German painters of the second half of the fifteenth century. Several characteristics of his style are beyond all comparions because they were exclusively typical, and for the first time, of Flemish art and later, in the fifteenth century, of art as practised north of the Alps. One of these characteristics of style, which constituted a main factor in the development of the new oil technique, was the artist's effort to engage himself entirely in the reproduction of each detail in order to portray as faithfully as possible nature, including the characterization of surfaces, something which the Italians have never attempted. Another typical peculiarity was Jan's overriding need to portray all his figures as individuals. His art as a portrait-painter was, at that time, an isolated phenomenon in Europe.

L. BALDASS
Jan van Eyck, 1952.

Van Eyck saw the world in its details and very closely, but in his picture he succeeded in giving unity to this variety of analytical elements. This unity was based partly upon a conquest of his vision: light; and partly upon his decorative feeling for the distribution of his masses of color.

A. PHILIPPOT
Examination of the picture before its restoration. In *The Adoration of the Sacred Lamb in the laboratory*, 1953.

BIBLIOGRAPHICAL NOTE

The bibliographical sources on Jan Van Eyck consist of more or less extensive quotations from Ciriaco de' Pizzicolli of Ancona (about 1450), Bartolomeo Facio (about 1450), Antonio di Piero Averulino, called *Il Filarete* (1465), Giovanni Santi (about 1490), Hieronymus Münzer (1495), Jean Lemaire de Belges (1504–11), Antonio de Beatis (1517), and Albrecht Dürer (1521). The following should be consulted: G. Vasari, *Le Vite*, Florence, 1550 (Second Edition 1568); L. de Heere, *Den Hof en Boomgaerd der Poësien*, Gand 1565; L. Guicciardini, *Descrittione di tutti i Paesi Bassi*, Antwerp 1567; M. van Vaernewijck, *Spieghel der Nederlandscher Audthevt*, Antwerp 1568 (seven successive editions: *Historie van Belgis*); J. Marchantius, *Flandria descripta*, Antwerp 1596; C. van Mander, *Het Schilderboeck*, Haarlem 1604, P. Opmeer, *Opus chronographicum orbis universi*, Antwerp 1611; A. Sanderus; *Flandria illustrata*, Cologne 1641.

Among the most important modern works, the following should also be consulted:

K. VOLL. *Die Werke des Jan Van Eyck*, Strasburg 1900.

K. VOLL. "Altes und Neues über die Brüder Eyck," in *Repertorium für Kunstwissenschaft* 1900.

W. H. J. WEALE. *Hubert and John Van Eyck, their Life and Work*, London 1908.

G. HULIN DE LOO. *Heures de Milan. Introduction historique*, Ghent 1911.

W. H. J. WEALE and M. W. BROCKWELL. *The Van Eycks and their Art*. London 1912.

M. CONWAY. *The Van Eycks and their Followers*, London 1912.

G. VAN DEN GHEYN. *L'interprétation du retable de St Bavon à Gand: l'Agneau Mystique des frères Van Eyck*, Brussels 1920.

M. J. FRIEDLÄNDER. *Der Genter Altar der Brüder Van Eyck*, Munich 1920.

A. SCHMARSOW. *Hubert und Jan Van Eyck*, Leipzig 1924.

F. WINKLER. *Altniederländische Malerei*, Berlin 1924.

M. J. FRIEDLNÄDER. *Die altniederländische Malerei*, Berlin 1924–37, vols. I and XIV.

M. DVORÀK. *Das Rätsel der Kunst der Brüder Van Eyck*, Munich 1925.

F. LYNA. "Uit en over handschriften. Het grafschrift van Hubrecht Van Eyck," in *De Kunst der Nederlander* 1930–1.

F. LYNA. *Over de echtheid van het grafschrift van Hubrecht Van Eyck en het quatrain van de Gentsche altaartafel*, Hassel 1933.

E. RENDERS. *Hubert Van Eyck, personnage de légende*, Paris-Brussels 1933.

J. DUVERGER. "Is Hubrecht een legendarisch personnage?" in *Kunst* 1933.

F. LYNA. *Een laatste rooord over het grafschrift van Hubrecht Van Eyck en over het Gentsche kroatrijn*, Hassel 1934.

E. RENDERS. *Jean Van Eyck*, Bruges 1935.

L. CLYSTERS. *Kunst en mystick, De aanbidding van het Lam*, Tongerlo 1935.

CH. DE TOLNAY. *Le retable de l'Agneau Mystique des Van Eyck*, Brussels 1938.

CH. DE TOLNAY. *Le Maître de Flémalle et les frères Van Eyck*, Brussels 1939.

H. BEENKEN. *Hubert und Jan Van Eyck*, Munich 1941.

J. DUVERGER. *Het grafschrift van Hubrecht Van Eyck en het quatrain van het Gentsche Lam Gods-retabel*, Antwerp-Utrecht 1945.

A. STUBBE. *Van Eyck en de gothiek*, Antwerp 1947.

A. ZILOTY. *La découverte de Jean Van Eyck et l'evolution du procédé à l'huile du Moyen-âge à nos jours*, Paris 1947.

E. RENDERS. *Jean Van Eyck et le polyptyque*, Brussels 1950.

L. BALDASS. *Jan Van Eyck*, London 1952.

P. COREMANS. *L'Agneau Mystique au Laboratoire*, Antwerp 1953.

REPRODUCTIONS

ACKNOWLEDGEMENT OF
PHOTOGRAPHS

Plates 7–72, 106–19, 122–7, and 156–60: *Archives Centrales Iconographiques d'Art National, Brussels*. Plates 73, 74 and 96–100: *Alinari, Florence*. Plates 102 and 103: *G. Hauck, Frankfurt*. Plates 128–30: *Anderson, Rome*. All other photographs have been kindly provided by the Galleries or Collections concerned.

ADORATION OF THE SACRED LAMB,
interior central panel. (*See plates 7–72*)

Plate 1. MADONNA IN A CHURCH, Berlin, Kaiser Friedrich Museum

Plate 2. *Detail of plate 1*

Plate 3. *Detail of plate 1*

Plate 4. STIGMATIZATION OF ST FRANCIS, Philadelphia, Pennsylvania Museum of Art

Plate 5. *Detail of plate 4*

Plate 6. *Detail of plate 4*

Plate 7. ADORATION OF THE SACRED LAMB,
Ghent, St Bavon Cathedral (*Outside*)

Plates 8–9. ADORATION OF THE SACRED LAMB (*Inside*)

Plate 10. THE SACRED LAMB: GOD

Plate 11. *Detail of plate 10*

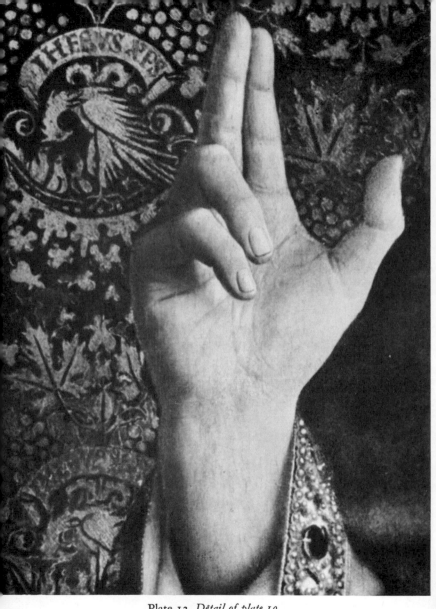

Plate 12. *Detail of plate 10*

Plate 13. *Detail of plate 10*

Plate 14. THE SACRED LAMB: THE VIRGIN

Plate 15. THE SACRED LAMB: JOHN THE BAPTIST

Plate 16. *Detail of plate 14*

Plate 17. *Detail of plate 15*

Plate 18. Detail of plate 10

Plate 19. *Detail of plate 15*

Plate 20. THE SACRED LAMB:
ANGELS PLAYING AND SINGING (*Left*)

Plate 21. THE SACRED LAMB:
ANGELS PLAYING AND SINGING (*Right*)

Plate 22. *Detail of plate 20*

Plate 23. *Detail of plate 21*

Plate 24. *Detail of plate 20*

Plate 25. *Detail of plate 21*

Plate 26. THE SACRED LAMB: TWO BIBLICAL EPISODES

Plate 27.
THE SACRED
LAMB: ADAM
AND EVE

Plate 28. *Detail of plate 27*

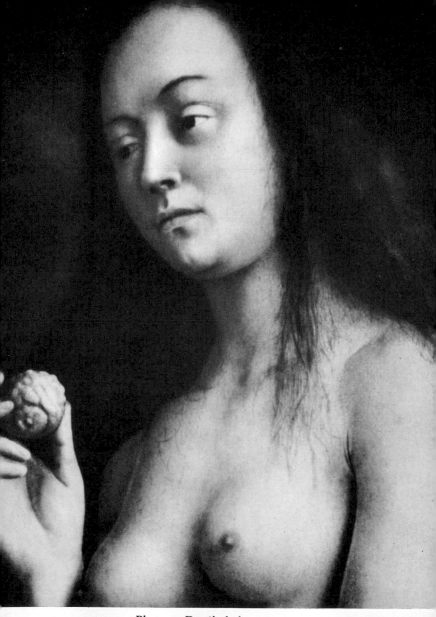

Plate 29. *Detail of plate 27*

Plate 30. *Detail of plate 27*

Plate 31. *Detail of plate 27*

Plates 32–33. THE SACRED LAMB, INNER
CENTRAL PANEL: THE ADORATION

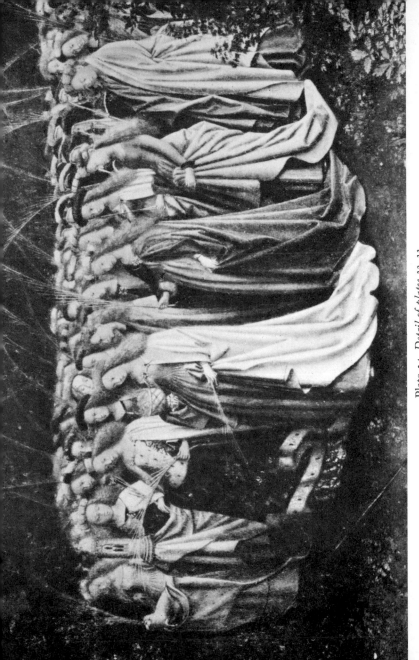

Plate 34. Detail of plates 32–33

Plate 35. *Detail of plates 32–33*

Plate 36. Detail of plates 32–33

Plate 37. *Detail of plates 32–33*

Plate 38. *Detail of plates 32–33*

Plate 39. *Detail of plates 32–33*

Plate 40. *Detail of plates 32–33*

Plate 41. *Detail of plates 32–33*

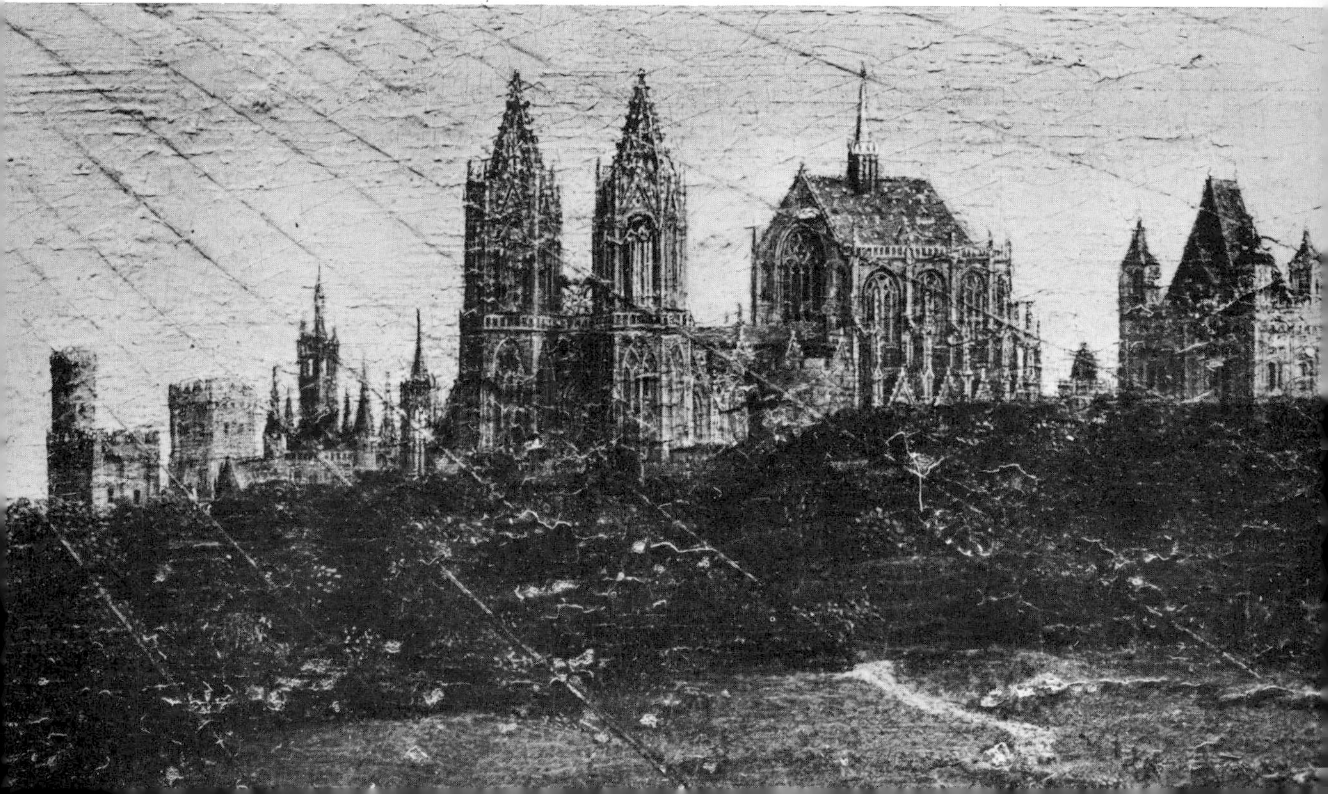

Plate 42. *Detail of plates 32–33*

Plate 43. *Detail of plates 32–33*

Plate 44. *Detail of plates 32–33*

Plate 45. *Detail of plates 32–33*

Plate 46. THE SACRED LAMB: JUST JUDGES AND KNIGHTS OF CHRIST

Plate 47. THE SACRED LAMB: HERMITS AND PILGRIMS

Plate 48. *Detail of plate 46*

Plate 49. *Detail of plate 47*

Plate 50. *Detail of plate 46*

Plate 51. *Detail of plate 46*

Plate 52. *Detail of plate 47*

Plate 53. *Detail of plate 47*

Plate 54. *Detail of plate 47*

Plate 55. *Detail of plate 47*

Plate 56. THE SACRED LAMB: GABRIEL

Plate 57. THE SACRED LAMB: THE VIRGIN

Plate 58. *Detail of plate 56*

Plate 59. *Detail of plate 57*

Plate 60. THE SACRED LAMB: ZECHARIAH AND MICAH

Plate 61. THE SACRED LAMB: OUTER CENTRAL PANEL

Plate 62. *Detail of plate 61*

Plate 63. *Detail of plate 61*

Plate 64. *Detail of plate 61*

Plate 65. *Detail of plate 61*

IOHES BAP — IOHES EVAN

Plate 66. THE SACRED LAMB: JOHN THE BAPTIST AND
JOHN THE EVANGELIST

Plate 67. THE SACRED LAMB: THE DONOR AND HIS WIFE

Plate 68. *Detail of plate 66*

Plate 69. *Detail of plate 66*

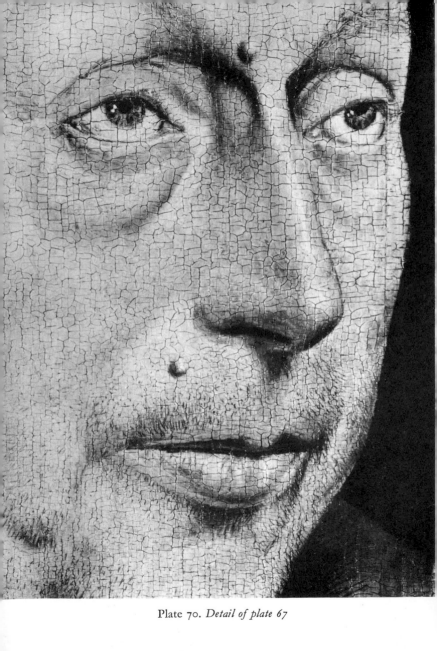

Plate 70. *Detail of plate 67*

Plate 71. *Detail of plate 67*

Plate 72. *Detail of plate 67*

PORTRAIT OF A YOUNG MAN
(detail)

Plate 73. CARDINAL ALBERGATI, Vienna, Kunsthistorisches Museum

Plate 74. *Detail of plate 73*

Plate 75. PORTRAIT OF A YOUNG MAN, London, National Gallery

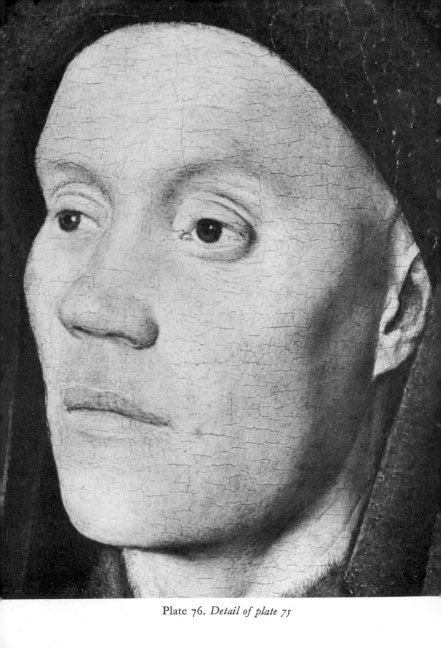

Plate 76. *Detail of plate 75*

Plate 77. MAN IN A TURBAN, London, National Gallery

Plate 78. *Detail of plate 77*

Plate 79. THE INCE HALL MADONNA,
Melbourne, National Gallery of Victoria

Plate 80. *Detail of plate 79*

Plate 81. ANNUNCIATION, Washington, National Gallery of Art

Plate 82. *Detail of plate 81*

Plate 83. *Detail of plate 81*

Plate 84. *Detail of plate 81*

Plate 85. *Detail of plate 81*

Plate 86. GIOVANNI ARNOLFINI, Berlin, Kaiser Friedrich Museum

Plate 87. THE MARRIAGE OF GIOVANNI ARNOLFINI
AND GIOVANNA CENAMI, London, National Gallery

Plate 88. *Detail of plate 87*

MAN IN A TURBAN

Plate 89. *Detail of plate 87*

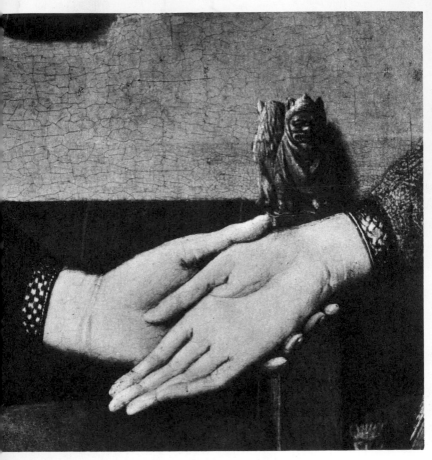

Plate 90. *Detail of plate 87*

Plate 91. *Detail of plate 87*

Plate 92. Detail of plate 87

Plate 93. *Detail of plate 87*

Plate 94. *Detail of plate 87*

Plate 95. *Detail of plate 87*

Plates 96–97. THE MADONNA TRIPTYCH,
Dresden, Gemäldegalerie (*Inside*)

Plate 98. *Detail of plates 96–97*

Plate 99. *Detail of plates 96–97*

Plate 100. THE MADONNA TRIPTYCH (*Outside*)

Plate 101. PORTRAIT OF A GOLDSMITH,
Rumania, Baron Bruckenthal Collection

Plate 102. THE LUCCA MADONNA, Frankfurt, Staedel Institute

Plate 103. *Detail of plate 102*

Plate 104. ANNUNCIATION: GABRIEL,
Lugano, Von Thyssen Collection

Plate 105. ANNUNCIATION: THE VIRGIN,
Lugano, Von Thyssen Collection

Plate 106. VIRGIN WITH CHANCELLOR ROLIN, Paris, Louvre

Plate 107. *Detail of plate 106*

Plate 108. *Detail of plate 106*

Plate 109. *Detail of plate 106*

Plate 110. *Detail of plate 106*

Plate III. VIRGIN WITH CANON VAN DER PAELE, Bruges, Schone Kunsten Museum

Plate 112. *Detail of plate 111*

Plate 113. *Detail of plate III*

Plate 114. *Detail of plate 111*

Plate 115. *Detail of plate 111*

Plate 116. *Detail of plate 111*

Plate 117. *Detail of plate 111*

Plate 118. *Detail of plate 111*

Plate 119. *Detail of plate 111*

Plate 120. JAN DE LEEUW,
Vienna, Kunsthistorisches Museum

Plate 121. BALDOVINO DE LANNOY,
Berlin, Kaiser Friedrich Museum

Plate 122. ST BARBARA, Antwerp, Schone Kunsten Museum

Plate 123. *Detail of plate 122*

Plate 124. THE VIRGIN AT THE FOUNTAIN,
Antwerp, Schone Kunsten Museum

Plate 125. *Detail of plate 124*

Plate 126. MARGHARITA VAN EYCK,
Bruges, Schone Kunsten Museum

Plate 127. *Detail of plate 126*

Plate 128. THE THREE MARYS AT THE SEPULCHER,

Plate 129. *Detail of plate 128*

Plate 130. *Detail of plate 128*

os autem gloriari oportet in cruce dmi
nostri ihesu xpristi in quo est salus uita
et resurrectio nostra per quem saluati
liberati sumus . ps. deus misereatur

Plate 131. TURIN BOOK OF HOURS: DISCOVERY OF THE CROSS,
Turin, Museo Civico (*attrib.*)

Plate 132. TURIN BOOK OF HOURS: REQUIEM MASS (*attrib.*)

Plate 133. TURIN BOOK OF HOURS: BIRTH OF ST JOHN (*attrib.*)

Plate 134. TURIN BOOK OF HOURS: illuminated capital letter (*attrib.*)

Plate 135. TURIN BOOK OF HOURS: illuminated capital letter (*attrib.*)

Plate 136. CRUCIFIXION *and* THE LAST JUDGEMENT,
New York, Metropolitan Museum of Art (*attrib.*)

Plate 137. *Detail of plate 136*

Plate 138. *Detail of plate 136*

Plate 139. *Detail of plate 136*

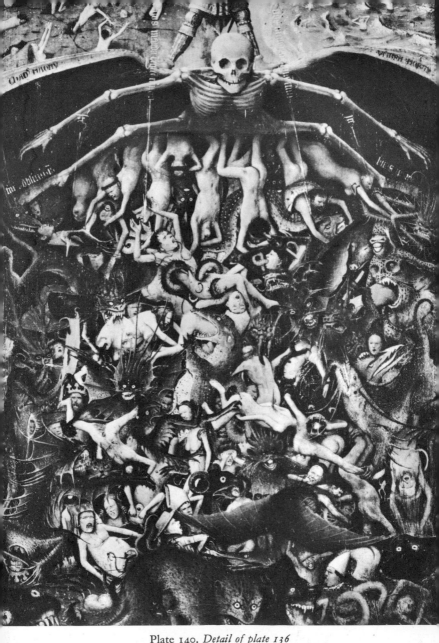

Plate 140. *Detail of plate 136*

Plate 141. CRUCIFIXION, Berlin, Kaiser Friedrich Museum (*attrib.*)

Plate 142. *Detail of plate 141*

Plate 143. MADONNA WITH TWO SAINTS AND CARTHUSIAN MONK,
Paris, Rothschild Collection (*attrib.*)

Plate 144. ANNUNCIATION,
New York, Metropolitan Museum of Art (*attrib*.)

Plate 145. *Detail of plate 144*

Plate 146. ST JEROME STUDYING, De__oit, Institute of Arts (*attrib.*)

Plate 147. VIRGIN WITH ABBOT VAN MAELBEKE,
Paris, Private Collection (*attrib.*)

Plate 148. HEAD OF CHRIST, British Private Collection (*attrib.*)

Plate 149. HEAD OF CHRIST, Berlin, Kaiser Friedrich Museum (*attrib.*)

Plate 150. ECCLESIASTIC,
Montauban, Ingres Museum (*attrib.*)

Plate 151. PORTRAIT OF A MAN,
Philadelphia, Pennsylvania Museum of Art (*attrib.*)

Plate 152. FRAGMENT OF A DONOR,
Leipzig, Bildende Künste Museum (*attrib.*)

Plate 153. MAN HOLDING PINK,
Berlin, Kaiser Friedrich Museum (*attrib.*)

Plate 154. *Detail of plate 153*

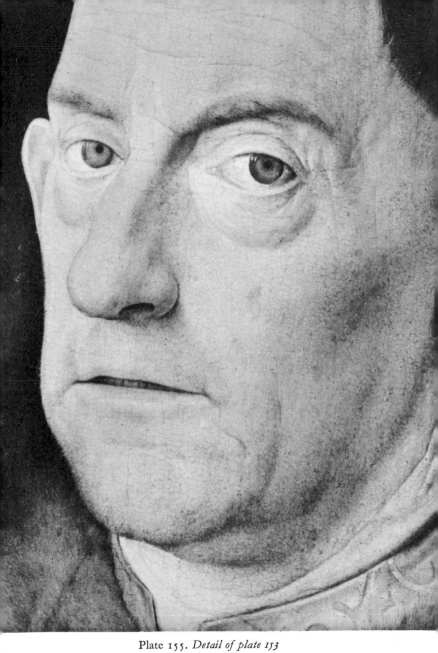

Plate 155. *Detail of plate 153*

Plate 156. STIGMATIZATION OF ST FRANCIS,
Turin, Galleria Sabauda (*attrib*).

Plate 157. *Detail of plate 156*

Plate 158. *Detail of plate 156*

Plate 159. *Detail of plate 156*

Plate 160. *Detail of plate 156*

LIBRARY
JUNIOR COLLEGE DISTRICT
ST. LOUIS, MO.

INVENTORY 74

COMPLETED

INVENTORY 1983